MARKETING YOUR BUSINESS COLLECTION

FACEBOOK ADVERTISING

THE ULTIMATE GUIDE

A Complete Step-By-Step Method With Smart And Proven Internet Marketing Strategies

WRITTEN BY

DALE CROSS

no scenarios in which the publisher or the original author of this work can be in any fashion deemed liable for any hardship or damages that may befall them after undertaking information described herein.

Additionally, the information in the following pages is intended only for informational purposes and should thus be thought of as universal. As befitting its nature, it is presented without assurance regarding its prolonged validity or interim quality. Trademarks that are mentioned are done without written consent and can in no way be considered an endorsement from the trademark holder.

CONTENTS

INTRODUCTION

Facebook is one of the quickest developing sites on the Internet, and because of its gigantic user base, it very well may be a great way to advertise your business. It may not be appropriate for everybody, but preferably there are certain sorts of companies that can truly benefit from advertising on Facebook.

A great many people have seen Google's adverts, a set of pay-per-click adverts which can be overseen through the Google AdWords tool. It's an extremely viable way of advertising to people that are completing a search in Google for the product or service that you offer. Facebook likewise runs a fundamentally the same as sort of advertising, taking a shot at a pay-per-click premise that you can set a financial plan for.

So for what reason would you think about advertising on Facebook, as opposed to Google or elsewhere on the internet? All things considered, when people utilize search motors to search for a specific product, they typically know mainly what it is that they need to find. Nonetheless, a few businesses have a product or service that people wouldn't go searching for, yet they would love on the off chance that they found it. On the off chance that the product that you offer fits this portrayal, at that point, you could truly benefit from an advertising campaign on Facebook.

Inside our business, we offer business coaching services where we coach and tutor proprietors of private ventures. Bunches of people in the industry aren't mindful of business coaching or don't completely comprehend it, and there are not very many that would go out looking currently searching for a business coh. In any case, they went over one and discovered precisely ho we could assist them with their business; they may find that it's a significant service that they would never have thought to search out for themselves.

Along these lines, where Google exceeds expectations at search, Facebook is great for revelation. Furthermore, it works splendidly on the off chance that you have another, personal product, or you're a business that is privately orientated. People love to find nearby businesses that they genuinely appreciate working with and Facebook gives you a chance.

For instance, say you're a neighborhood store. At the point when people find your shop, they love you and your grand scope of pickles and chutneys entirely. Usually, they'll need to inform their companions concerning you since they've discovered a great place!

On the off chance that you get a great deal of your business through proposals, similar to this, you may be the sort of activity where Facebook advertising can work exceptionally well for you.

There are 600 million users on Facebook, and the span of the user base alone empowers you to get in front of a considerable crowd possibly. The magnificence of Facebook is that you can pinpoint precisely who you need to see your adverts. You can target people in a quite specific area with the goal that your ads show up for people who are based near you. You can choose whether your adverts show up based on sexual orientation, relationship status, and even the pages that the user has effectively Liked. This gives you the inconceivable capacity to take advantage of your target market. So in case you're a goldsmith in Birmingham for instance, we can set up a Facebook advertising campaign where your ads would show for men, somewhere in the range of 25 and 35, who are in a relationship, yet not locked in or not wedded, inside the Birmingham area. Facebook advertising is an excellent and efficient way of getting in front of the people that you are attempting to reach.

CHAPTER ONE

How to Use Facebook Advertising for Your Business

Within excess of 400 million clients, Facebook is an excellent place for business owners to increase some superb permeability, and that permeability can be targeted to a particular audience. Without a doubt, a great many people consider Facebook a place to keep in contact with companions, however business owners understand the estimation of Facebook advertising. Merely investigate the right sidebar on any Facebook page, and you will perceive what I mean. Those Facebook notices are set up to get you, the targeted audience to investigate what that business brings to the table, and has been set up to be viewed by the same number of or few as wanted.

Here is a little data about how you can utilize Facebook advertising to help fabricate your own particular business.

Target your Audience

One incredible element of Facebook advertising is that you can set it up to be viewed by a chosen group of people. That could be by age or sex and also geographic territory. You can likewise set up your target audience as indicated by training, workplace, and relationship status. Catchphrases are another way to target your audience while using Facebook management strategies.

After you have settled on your audience, you should determine where you need to coordinate your potential customers. That could be to your site or an offshoot interface. It could likewise be to a lead catch page on the off chance that you are building a rundown.

Settle on Your Advertising Budget

Facebook advertising should be possible on a cost for every click or cost per thousand premises. Research has been done on the viability of every one of these models, and it appears that the cost per click is the ideal way to get the most profit for your venture.

When you start your campaign, you should settle on an everyday spending plan and set your Facebook management to that number. Once that number has been accomplished, your advertisement won't be appealed to some other users. These numbers can be balanced as you determine the viability of your publication.

Test Your Advertising

It doesn't make a difference where you are spending your advertising cash; you ought to always test to make beyond any doubt that you have made savvy speculation. Facebook advertising is the same. By creating various ads and putting everyone on your Facebook management tool, you will have the capacity to see which ones are best, and when that is determined, you will have the ability to drop those that are not performing admirably. It could be simple as changing the picture to draw in the attention of your audience that makes the distinction between ads.

The Next Step is Analysis

Facebook advertising enables you to dissect how your ads are getting along with the Facebook Insights tool. This tool will assist you with bettering understand the interests and socioeconomics of the individuals who are clicking on your ads, and which watchwords got their advantage.

Better Facebook management is the way to progress for your business in this Internet marketing world.

What's the Best Approach to Facebook Advertising?

Facebook Advertising Methods That are the Most Effective

Facebook happens to be the greatest interpersonal organization today, with positively no considerable rivalry. The absolute nearness of Facebook makes it a blessing from heaven for advertisers. With a large number of dynamic users that can be laser targeted, advertising on Facebook is the thing that you ought to do in case you're not. Regardless of what sort of thing you need to offer or attract attention to, you'll discover an audience for it inside Facebook's users. The following section gives you an understanding of what Facebook can improve the situation you and how you can use this new advertising platform in an ideal way.

Read the advertiser guidelines for Facebook thoroughly. This is vital because on the off chance that you don't understand the tenets or guidelines it is less demanding to damage them and get stuck in an unfortunate situation or prohibited which makes it hard to hold your advertising in line. Bunches of people who are beginner advertisers on Facebook locate their individual and advertising campaigns in a dangerous position since they didn't follow the specific, straightforward principles set forward by Facebook. Since Facebook's system is enormous, the organization has set up strict tenets and controls for advertisers to keep things in place - so it just makes sense to follow the guidelines that are spread out.

If you utilize a unique landing page for the people clicking on your Facebook ads, at that point make beyond any doubt, you center around growing an email list by using a press page. People will probably make a buy on the off chance that they know you and more averse to purchase the first occasion when they see a sales page, which is the reason sending people straight to a sales page is less convincing. Swinging supporters of clients are substantially simpler than somebody making a buy the first occasion when they arrive on your page. Each Internet advertiser knows the estimation of follow up marketing, where you intend to follow up with your prospects and endeavor to bring the deal to a close. It additionally passes by "dribble marketing."

You additionally need your ads to produce a high click-through rate, because a higher CTR will mean a lower cost for each click for that advertisement. Much the same as AdWords, even Facebook has a similar sort of principles for deciding the execution of an advertisement. So merely ahead and try out different pictures with your ads to see which one gives the best results. This should be possible by ensuring your ads are targeted at various age groups and presented the results figuring out which group is more suited for your income targets. It's easy to understand that on the off chance that you need to get however much as could reasonably be expected out of Facebook's advertising that you have to concentrate the more significant part of your attention on things like the way your ads get made, the nature of the item you need to advance and how high your landing page is. So what everything comes down to is the approach you take with every one of the campaigns you need to run. The main thing that you have to remember is that Facebook like some other advertising platform has an expectation to absorb information, yet that doesn't mean you won't discover accomplishment with it. Just make some move, and see the results coming your way.

3 Competitive Advantages That Businesses Can Leverage With Facebook Advertising

Better Customer Targeting

Facebook offers a remarkable chance of setting ads to reach more than 500 million dynamic clients in a single place. It doesn't get more streamlined than this. You can without much of a stretch select your target gathering of people by pinpointing the age, area, and interests you might want to speak to. You can likewise test basic picture and content-based ads to perceive what works best and respond in like manner.

Strengthen Your Relationships with Consumers and Gain New Relationships

You can utilize ad placement on Facebook to advertise your company Facebook page or company website, and since you can target your gathering of people so well with Facebook, you can create more significant leads and guests than any time in recent memory. This is likewise an extraordinary way to manufacture and strengthen a network around your business and become your following speedier than any time in recent memory. Utilizing the "Like" catch highlight through Facebook, which is accessible for ads, is additionally essential to building your online notoriety.

Budget Control

Facebook advertising has been known to be more affordable than other marketing devices and is additionally fantastically adaptable to accommodate your budget necessities. You have the option to set the day by day budget you are mostly OK with and adjust your budget at any given time should the need for change emerge. PPC (pay per click) is an option you can use with your Facebook ad placement, where you don't pay except if somebody clicks on your ad or you can pay per every thousand impressions. Facebook's scope of adoptions makes ad placement more moderate and compelling than any other time in recent memory.

In any case that you are searching for a matter of a company that prevailing with a Facebook ad campaign, take CM Photographics for example. They burned through $600 in advertising on Facebook and chose to target women whose Facebook statuses noticed that they were engaged. Over a year timeframe, CM Photographics produced nearly $40,000 in income from a minor $600 marketing campaign! The transformation was fundamentally astonishing as 60% of the clients coordinated to CM Photographic's website ended up qualified leads. Who can contend with results this way?

Advertising on Facebook has undoubtedly turned out to be an inexpensive and unimaginably powerful marketing system. It's unfathomably adaptable, customized, and if utilized appropriately can stretch out your company's reach to more potential clients than you would ever envision. Substantial or little company, gigantic or minute advertising budget, cell phone sales or summer bathing suits - your company ought not to leave behind this one of a kind and productive advertising opportunity.

Subject: Facebook Advertising - 3 Tips for Maximum Results

Facebook advertising has been known as the "AdWords Killer" and touted as the Next Big Thing in Internet Marketing.

Like this, a million and one "masters" have jumped up out of the woodwork, each professing to have the One True Secret to successful Facebook advertising.

Facebook Advertising...

Is nothing on a fundamental level "new." It's only another way of completing an old thing, and all the whine merely is people hopping on a passing trend. This pattern is just the same old thing new and is quite depressingly well-known because it happens each time something new goes along.

However, the fundamental truth is... Facebook Advertising is about the Return On Investment, your ROI. That is it. All the rest is merely hot air and wind.

It likewise implies agonizing over the "cost" of Facebook advertising is good for nothing except if you know how much it's making you. Furthermore, if it costs you short of what you're making in sales as a result, at that point, it's worth doing.

What's more, that is about more or less troublesome - you don't need a master to reveal to all of you that, isn't that so?

In this way, here are three basic hints to guarantee you're getting the best results you can get from your Facebook advertising:

Target the correct gathering. Don't be lured by getting your ad before substantial quantities of people. Keep in mind, being successful isn't tied in with getting the most astounding number of clicks - it's tied in with amplifying your ROI. What you need are clicks from profoundly qualified people not clicks merely fundamentally. In case you're a nearby store, and you offer locally (say, you're a beautician) at that point target your geological zone as nearly as possible; on the off chance that you have practical experience in offering marriage wear, target women who are engaged, et cetera.

Test, test and afterward test some more. Don't merely hurl an ad and anticipate that it will be successful the first time. Be substance to get A result - it doesn't considerably matter how high or dangerous it is. Since the thought is to write TWO ads and see which one does best. At that point, write a third ad and test it against the best of the initial two; at that point write a fourth ad and check it against the best of the initial three, et cetera. Along these lines, you can rapidly and effectively increment your Click Through Rate and abatement your Cost Per Click.

Change over! Getting clicks is just the primary portion of the condition. To influence it to pay, you need to change over clicks to purchasers! So you need to buckle down on your presentation pages AND watch your transformation rates like a falcon. Also, this is the thing that makes your CPC relatively unimportant - on the off chance that you know a website guest is worth all things considered $20, at that point paying $10 to get a click isn't expensive.

The truth is, Facebook advertising has incredible potential, yet like any advertising you need to realize what you're doing, as well as need to comprehend a fundamental marketing truth which applies to ALL types of advertising and marketing, from the humblest postcard to the most complex online pay-per-click advertising campaign.

Does Facebook Advertising Work? Well, That Depends - Read On To Find Out

Promoting ideas and business names on Facebook may appear like an inquisitive idea. A few advertisers may think about how the idea functions and how much the advancement will cost. Systems administration sites are by, and fat blasting with people perusing them, and promoting ideas and ideas on these sites could guarantee that numerous people are presented to it. Does Facebook advertising work for everybody and their needs? The appropriate response may rely upon the type of business that is being advanced. Each company will have their unique methods for achieving their target audiences.

Demonstrated Process

Marketing angles have been a good idea of in the realm of Facebook. They have a novel advertising strategy that works for them, their users and their advertising companies. The framework is set up with the goal that everybody in the process wins.

Is it Free?

People might be shocked to discover that advertising on the web with Facebook is in reality free. Facebook does not charge to post an advertisement on their pages. Ads can be set on a landing page, or a profile page has a place with a specific user. It doesn't cost any money to put an advertisement on someone's page, the central time that someone needs to pay is the point at which someone clicks on the promotion. People can see the development without clicking on it and still get an unmistakable message about what it is.

PPC - Pay Per Click

The way that the systems administration site profits are by charging per clicks onto each site. Promoters will be charged for the occasions that someone clicks on their advertisement. That implies that if they have a day where nobody clicks on their promotion, they don't need to pay. Business scenes need to pay for the aggregate number of times that their ads are clicked on and seen. That can be extremely cost proficient for marketing companies. It can likewise enable companies to know who is clicking on their ads and which ones are not creating any clicks.

The Targets

Business owners can likewise target particular groups of people and sexual orientation. If someone has an item or administration to offer, they may make their very own settings for advertising the thing. An application is rounded out that will contain the more significant part of the coveted information. For instance, the business proprietor may ask for that lone females are targeted and that they are between a specific age group. This sort of targeted advertising can guarantee that the correct group of people is focused.

Another bright idea that Facebook has with their promoters is that they can get to information about their users and fans. The information that is picked up can be utilized to target particular companies. People who have a pet company will get the chance to focus on people who possess or love creatures. If someone has photos of their pet on their profile or has creature groups recorded as their interests, at that point they might be sent any promotion that needs to do with creatures.

Families who have children may find that they get a great deal of family and kid-related commercial. Facebook administrators will discover that the user is keen on kids and will utilize that information to target specific companies. Companies that arrangement with family administrations and tyke exercises might be directed toward their social pages.

The most effective method to Save Money With Facebook Advertising.

Here are a couple of strategies that you can save money by utilizing Facebook advertising:

1. Utilize the cost per impression setting versus the cost per click setting

You should pay less for advertising costs when utilizing the cost per impression setting insofar as you are getting a decent click-through rate.

2. Direct your clicks to your Facebook page

If you direct your clicks to your Facebook page instead of to your external website, your cost per click will probably be less costly. The one thing that despite everything you need to do is to ensure your Facebook page is set up just like your website in that you can have guests join to your rundown and you are likewise set up to send them through your business channel.

3. Just keep your ads dynamic for a day or two

When you initially begin your Facebook advertising, you get the more significant part of your clicks on the specific first or second day. Your target audience becomes accustomed to seeing your ads throughout the following couple of days, and they don't click on them to such an extent. What you ought to do will be to switch up your ads each other day with new headlines and new pictures. Doing this, you surely will keep up the enthusiasm of your audience. Create an adequate measure of these varieties for around multi-month or thereabouts and afterward begin again with the first promotion and continue turning the rest through in a cycle. You would make a series of ads rather than just a single development. Similar to part testing. Like this, your ads don't get stale, and your audience will remain intrigued by what you are advertising.

Monitor which ads are playing out the best and once you have burned through your series, keep the ones that did the best and run them once more. Continue adding to the series with various headlines, distinctive photographs, and diverse advertisement content. You need to keep your cost per click down under $.30 per click.

4. Would you be able certainly if you are profiting?

To learn precisely how much money, you are making or losing utilizing Facebook advertising, you need to track everything. It is essential for you to follow the cost per click, the click-through rate, and what level of those clicks are buying into your fan page or transforming into leads by going to your website. You additionally must have a useful deals pipe set up while catching your points. You could genuinely have the ideal click-through rate, and you could be producing points, notwithstanding if nobody is purchasing anything, you are losing money.

Adverting on Facebook can be significantly more remunerating than Google AdWords. The type of advertising that you do on Facebook, which is practically a delicate offer approach, is dominant on Facebook. This type of strategy can't work successfully on Google AdWords. Also, the cost per click could well be extensively more on Google AdWords than on Facebook.

These are just a couple of strategies that you can save money when advertising on Facebook as opposed to advertising with Google AdWords. Merely recollect, while utilizing these strategies, track everything that you can so you can decide exactly how much money you are making using Facebook advertising.

Is Facebook Advertising Free? The Question Most People Ask

For any business that needs to extend and advance their business, interpersonal organizations give a proper and straightforward way contact a more extensive gathering of people. Facebook has increased enormous use everywhere throughout the world, and along these lines, this has made it the ideal advertising decision for general businesses. In any case, is Facebook advertising free? This is the issue that the vast majority solicit given the considerable expense of advertising particularly in conventional media. With an incredible supporter base of more than 500 million users, Facebook would be required to make a fortune out of advertising. Half of these supporters are generally online for a normal of an hour daily. With such bewildering measurements, Facebook is an ideal ground for advertisers, especially those businesses that have taken to web-based promoting. What is significantly more unimaginable is that advertising on Facebook is completely free! Anyway, how is Facebook advertising for free? Especially considering the substantial net revenues announced by Facebook every year?

The easy way to find a solution to this inquiry is by following the simple steps talked about beneath on the best way to open a Facebook business page. In any case, numerous people will, in any case, ponder whether there would anything say anything is free on the web and still ask a similar inquiry: is Facebook advertising free? Above all else, it will be savvy to dissect these simple steps that take after right away. On the Facebook login page, diverse classes of making a page are accessible. These incorporate business, craftsman, organization, amusement, brand or cause of network. A business page will fall in the business or organization option in the rundown. This category causes a business to rank high in typical Facebook looks. After choosing the characterization, the following stage is to round out the business name and other information that relates to the business. For accuracy, a business logo might be fitting and is uploaded in the following step. After this is finished, Facebook will give an option to welcome companions. An incite for filling essential information will then show up. This is the place information like business website URL, and a concise portrayal is filled. This part is open and can center around the product, system, brand et cetera.

The information can be altered by clicking on the 'Alter data' option. More information about the business, for example, working hours can be added here. At long last, clicking on a business hyper-connect distributes the business page. Users would then be able to be welcome to 'like' the page and can impact their companions to like the page likewise since it shows up on their profile. As basic as the system is by all accounts, it puts a business on the worldwide social guide completely for free. The inquiry 'Is Facebook advertising free?' has been replied with the simple steps of making a Facebook business page. Having made the business page and imparted it to users, it is anything but challenging to broadcast products, administrations, offers, and advancements. Numerous different thoughts can be coordinated to fuseways of introducing a business in the ideal way conceivable. Earnestly, is Facebook advertising free? Indeed, and companies should exploit this.

5 Tips to Improve Your Facebook Advertising

We as a whole know Facebook is a crucial advertising instrument for general businesses. Regularly, being on Facebook isn't sufficient, as, you may experience considerable difficulties inspiring people to tail you. Facebook advertising could be an exceptionally financially savvy way to build up a following, yet, with a specific end goal to do as such, you should ensure your ad is upgraded. In this section, we diagram 5 essential tips to advance your Facebook advertising.

Before you make your advertisement, you should choose your identity targeting. Facebook is handy in that it enables you to target your showcasing to people on Facebook in light of their preferences, status, sexual orientation, area, and so on. This targeted advertising is sufficient to ensure your ad achieves your target statistic. You can execute the accompanying tips to your Facebook ad to enhance the odds of getting took note:

1. Use a colored border around your picture to inspire it to emerge

Whenever you sign on to Facebook, you see those advertisements in the right-hand segment, in any case, your eye is prepared to center around your course of events and not by any means meander to one side of the page. Utilizing a system, for example, putting a solid red or colored border around your picture will tend to attract the eye to your advertisement and increment the odds of getting the saw and having another devotee click through to your profile.

2. Use a video as your advertisement

Studies have exhibited that a champion among the best ways to advance a product is through video. Many individuals tend to click through to use videos, along these lines, if you have a video that discussions about your business, use the connection to the video as your Facebook advertisement.

3. Have your advertisement keep running on fan pages of your competitors or integral businesses

On the off chance that you have competitors that are maintaining a comparable business to yours, what preferred the group of onlookers to catch over those supporters that you know have a personal stake in your company. Having your advertisement show up on the fan pages of your competitors, or a correlative business is an incredible way to drive the correct devotees to your site.

4. Think about advertising amid the nights

Nighttimes can be less expensive and more advantageous to advertise because of a couple of reasons. To begin with, you have less competition as the financial plans of numerous organizations gets used up amid the day. Second, while many individuals are checking their Facebook amid the daytime from work, they tend to be less focused. Amid the night, when at home, loose, more people are probably going to take as much time as is needed glancing through Facebook and have an expanded capacity to focus.

5. Use a QR code instead of a picture as your advertisement

While QR codes have not been taken off in the way, they were required to do, utilizing QR codes as your advertisement picture could get you free advertising. On the off chance that an individual uses their advanced cell to examine your system, you don't pay for the click through. This could be a vital component of extending your financial plan.

Facebook Advertising for Small Business Owners

Facebook Advertising Introduction

In the present chapter, we will talk about Facebook PPC advertising and give a few hints and little-known techniques for small business owners. Facebook pay per click enables you to target a chose area so if you are a small business proprietor with a shop, you can cast a net to just the areas you overhauled. This will enable tight to down your targeting and ensure quality leads. Facebook pay per click chips away at an offering framework. The cost you pay per click you get relies upon your offer, the specialty, and the nature of your ad and the website you are advertising. Having quality substance is an absolute necessity, recall when you are composing your content to keep in touch with users, and not to the PC.

Composing your Facebook Ad

Facebook permits two options, on the off chance that you have a Facebook page for your business, you can advertise the page correctly, or you can advertise a website straightforwardly. Contingent upon what you are endeavoring to develop, however for our motivations we will center around announcing a Facebook page because I think they are somewhat more straightforward. Recorded beneath are the options we need to set with a specific end goal to advertise a Facebook page.

Ensure you have a headline that POPS! Your headline is likely the most vital piece of your ad, the picture being the second. Having excellent Ad Copy is an absolute requirement with regards to composing ads. Keep in mind you are competing with different business owners in your area who additionally need customers. You must be forceful.

Targeting customers on Facebook

When you claim a shop, advertising will be a little unique when utilizing pay per click. The huge advantage is as that you can target a particular area as I expressed previously. When you are a business with a shop and a website that offers products, at that point you can advertise to places outside of your area if you wish. This is an extraordinary way to investigate and find new customers. On the off chance that your business does not work in a specific area then different principles apply.

First, let's talk about users with a physical shop. Users who work in a particular area would profit best by targeting people in a specific radius of their business. I recommend you make a rundown of how you're going to target your customers. I will use a pet shop for instance business. A pet shop in York PA with no website would begin their targeting list by targeting the York PA Area, or potentially a couple encompasses districts. Next thing on Facebook we need to investigate the age and sexual orientation. Contingent upon your product, these options will be set quickly. For our pet shop purposes, we will Focus on people who are between the ages of 30-50. Next category will be particular intrigue. Since we are a pet shop, lets target #Animal Planet. Attempt to be innovative when your targeting. Facebook additionally offers a Broad Category area where you can be more particular about your targeting options. The following is an example of what our targeting would resemble.

Three Ways to Make Your Facebook Advertising More Effective

Once in a while, another type of advertising hits the scene, and as far as the web the most recent thing getting everybody talking is Facebook advertising. Numerous web specialists are stating Facebook advertising may one day be more significant than Google AdWords, and there are presently many Facebook advertising courses jumping up, every one promising to demonstrate to you the key to utilizing this new advertising medium.

In any case, even though Facebook is a genuinely new medium, the way to use its advertising is entirely not quite the same as utilizing some other type of advertising media, because at last, it's only an alternate way of accomplishing something that has been around for quite a while. The most critical thing about any advertising is your return on investment, and anything else does not merit worrying about. The primary type of good advertising is beneficial advertising, and that means you need to spend not as much as the cash coming in. In case you're doing that, the advertising is fruitful, and you genuinely don't need to get the hang of anything else.

So how might you make beyond any doubt your Facebook advertising beneficial?

By following similar techniques, you use when utilizing some other type of advertising medium, that is the ticket.

1. **Focus on the correct people.** Regardless of which advertising framework you use, the advertising will fail if it's not going in front of the people interested in what you're offering. It's always better to have your advertisement going in front of fewer people who are qualified, rather than going in front of 10 times more people who are not interested in what you're offering by any means. This means focusing on people who are probably going to buy what you suggest. If you run a nearby store, make beyond any doubt you focus on your neighborhood geographic region. If you provide angling gear, put your advertisement in front of people who are interested in angling. This sounds straightforward, and it is, yet numerous businesses overlook this basic standard when they advertise and like this fail to get a return on investment.

2. **Watch out for transformations.** When you have people tapping on your ads, you need to make beyond any doubt they are changing over into sales or leads. This means you need to establish beyond any doubt your website pages are worked in the right way, and guide the peruser to precisely what you need them to do, either buying something or leaving their contact subtle elements so you can connect with them later. If you find you can burn through $50 on advertising, however, you wind up making $200 in sales, the advertising has more than paid for itself. Be that as it may, to get to this state you need to establish beyond any doubt your website pages are completing an appropriate activity.

3. **Continue testing constantly.** You'll always locate the first time you run ads, your prosperity rate will be genuinely low, and it's hugely only an instance of continue attempting unique methodologies and continually enhancing your actual visitor clicking percentage. Continue testing one promotion against another, quit utilizing the most exceedingly terrible one, and after that test the best one against another advertisement. Do this, and your ads will continually enhance, and you'll get a higher return on investment.

Facebook advertising can be an extraordinary way to get qualified leads and make sales. However, it will just work when you take after age-old standards of direct reaction advertising. Tossing cash at it won't go anyplace. You need to continually test your advertisements, and make beyond any doubt you're getting a return on investment, much the same as you would create some other gainful advertising effort.

Coordinate reaction marketing and lead age master Steve Prescott is the creator of Smart Business Power Marketing.

This report uncovers how web and customary marketing can incorporate to expand reaction rates and produce qualified leads. These methods have been tried in an extensive variety of business sectors as are relatively sure to work for you.

Straightforward Facebook Advertising and Marketing Ideas

Facebook advertising is a fantastic means to offer your administrations or things on the web. With the vast number of individuals on Facebook, it tends to be a genuine gold mine with regards to building your business. So in case you're interested in how to advertise and showcase your business on the web, you will need to peruse on.

The primary thing you need to do with regards to Facebook advertising and marketing is set up a Facebook account when you don't as of now have one. When you have set up your record and your page, you will need to create a fan page for your business opportunity. Keeping your page isolate from your business page is imperative. Along these lines, you won't disturb your loved ones with your business related posts. Your page must look proficient as this will be the central area a portion of your audience will see precisely what you bring to the table.

Next, you will need to start transferring material to your page. Make beyond any doubt the content you move on your Facebook advertising page is identified with your image name.

Desire your mates and household individuals to like your page and after that offer your data with their buddies and household. You could likewise provide a cost-free preliminary, an example, or a sale for the individuals who like your page.

When you start building up an audience, make posts that inclination your audience to respond. Get some information about their difficulties or post different other charming data that will motivate them to cooperate on your page. The more comments you have, the more others will need to participate in the fun a comment also. It is likewise an incredible way to keep them returning to your page.

Photos on your Facebook advertising and marketing page can be to a high degree accommodating. Facebook individuals are substantially more prone to comment on a picture than on content just post. The photos can likewise assist your post with standing out. Keep in mind that people will probably buy from or partner with somebody they trust. Discover what their difficulties are, furnish them with arrangements and pick up their trust.

Hold a challenge or give away a gift on your Facebook advertising page. This is a dynamite strategy to get individuals to your page to see precisely what you bring to the table and can incredibly improve your profit.

You don't need to distribute content pretty much your organization; you can likewise share content from different organizations or people that are in your particular specialty. By doing this, you are helping other individuals and driving much more activity to your website.

Facebook can be an extremely viable advertising gadget. Attempt the Facebook advertising suggestions shared underneath to get more activity and leads for your business.

Keep in mind that people will probably buy from or partner with somebody they trust. Discover what their difficulties are, furnish them with arrangements and pick up their trust.

Photos on your Facebook advertising and marketing page can be to a high degree advantageous. Hold a challenge or a gift on your Facebook advertising page.

13 Effective Facebook Advertising Tips You Can Start Implementing In Your Business

With over a billion active users month to month, Facebook is a road for social media marketing that is excessively tremendous, making it impossible to disregard! Notwithstanding, with the expanding decent variety of this social systems administration site, leaving an effect turns into merely more troublesome. In any case, don't fuss! With the right set of aptitudes and hardly enough innovativeness, formulating a strategy keeping in mind the end goal to get the most significant advantage out of Facebook turns out to be simple!

Recorded here are some Facebook advertising and marketing tips that you can use to help your execution for your business scalable. Through my Facebook Advertising Tips, you will figure out how to pick your campaign targets, comprehend the advantages of utilizing of an assortment of Facebook advertising formats and begin formulating a superior way to showcase what you have!

#1 Take the favorable position of Facebook ads while keeping your page engaging and progressive!

While it is imperative to advertise your business, it is similarly as vital to keeping up, if not increase, your believability. Numerous enterprises concentrate such a significant amount on Facebook ads that they begin to neglect their page. Remember that the page refreshes are similarly as central to your marketing endeavors as those clicks that you generate using ads!

Ads work best when combined with a fantastic timeline. Social media is certifiably not a straightforward matter of pulling inattention. Social media is tied in with connecting with individuals! Furthermore, what preferred the way to do that over having the ideal promotion to the perfect page!

#2 Bring inventive revolution into play.

Inventive revolution enables you to generate better exhibitions through persistent A/B testing. For the individuals who are not acquainted with the A/B test, this where you essentially test different advertisement duplicates, pictures and landing pages against each other. By making use of this system inside the newsfeed, you can invigorate messages, increase the click-through rate (CTR) and stay aware of the impression amounts! Hence, if you plan to quickly help your campaigns and make the more significant part of your Facebook endeavors, I'd propose you set up a framework based on a relentless revive of advertising messages.

#3 Utilize the correct page post format.

Each page post format has its own particular set of qualities and shortcomings. While choosing the most suitable form to utilize, manage in mind the target you wish to accomplish. In any case that you expect to generate site transformations or deals, choosing a "page post link" promotion would carry out the activity amazingly. In any case that you mean to propel mark association as your campaign goal, a "page post photo" advertisement might conceivably work.

Page post link ads appreciate a higher percent regarding change rate rather than page post photo ads. This is because you don't squander cash on clicks by individuals clicking on the picture. Instead, a page post link drives your guest straight to your landing page. Despite what might be expected, I have discovered page post photo ads generate a higher CTR rather than page post link ads. By understanding the distinction between the two formats, you can even join them to get the best out of the two universes!

#4 Set your goals and fittingly pick your line of assault.

The massive number of promotion openings given by Facebook can enable you to achieve your goals once you have set out the things you wish to accomplish. All that is left to do after figuring out what you need to reach is to get working. If your primary target is to produce mark mindfulness to develop a fan base, you might need in any case standard marketplace ads. Standard marketplace ads are explicitly linked to your Facebook page and enable Facebook users to like your page straight inside the advertisement unit. When you have an extensive fan base, you may likewise need to endeavor the use of a supported story, in which case a promotion comes up to companions who have enjoyed your page.

Regardless of what goal you have set your mind upon, or what strategy you have used, make beyond any doubt that you are situated to ascertain achievement!

#5 Set a target population.

Targeting a specific population or gathering with Facebook ads enables your advancement to continue significantly more efficiently. By setting a target population, you can elevate to the right users based on their real advantages, in this way expanding your prosperity rate. A target population requires not be constrained anyway to just those people whose interests are in line with your business. You can likewise target the companions of Facebook users who have beforehand enjoyed your page. If you want to advertise a particular post from your page, for example, a one of a kind offer or a unique news story, you can even make use of page post Sponsored Stories to switch your post into a newsfeed piece.

#6 Select photos that are sublime.

Infectious images will always pull in attention! The photos you select for your promotion are maybe among the most critical parts of snatching the watcher's advantage. While choosing an image to use, don't restrain yourself to your organization logo. Think about looking outside the standard however inside the extent of what you are putting forth.

In selecting photos, I have discovered the most amazing images for transformation are very much trimmed headshots. Only a tip. Do your best to avoid archetypal stock photos. Or maybe, endeavor to make use of more common images. Additionally, guarantee that the pictures you pick introduce themselves with hues that are discernable from the blue shading format of Facebook.

#7 Use Call to Action (CTA).

Because your promotion can comprise of up to 135 characters, doesn't mean you are required to use them all! Trust me; an extensive development does not involve a protracted rundown of clients. Every once in a while, a shorter line can work much better! In this way, in suitable circumstances, use an invitation to take action (CTA) that influences fans and users to click your advertisement. Along these lines, not exclusively does the ad convey a short and persuading message. However, it likewise illuminates the users concerning what activity you anticipate that they will perform when they get to your landing page.

#8 Produce and experiment with a few ads.

Don't just run a single promotion inside each campaign! Assorted variety can do you ponders! Even the littlest change in the words you select or the illustrations you utilize can outsized affect the CTR for your advertisement, so it's best to make various adjustments of your promotion and experiment with them to discover which ad gets the best reaction.

#9 Quotes shake! Make use of them as you esteem essential.

What could be hotter than a post to help up the day? Posts including moving or invigorating statements regularly perform exceptionally well, so don't be hesitant to use those inspiring words of astuteness. To zest things up, you can even connect a photo to your statement - shockingly better, do Pinterest-style image/quote overlay. An extraordinary free instrument I suggest for making eye getting picture cites a site named Canva.com. Individuals gobble that stuff up!

10 Allow users to embed their particular photo inscriptions.

Requesting users to give a subtitle to an energizing or snicker excellent photo is a savvy way to drive cooperation and commitment. What's more, it hits two winged creatures with one stone! It gets the user's attention and enables you to survey the viability of your marketing strategy.

11 Give motivating forces! Offer some particular substance to your Facebook fans.

Posting amazing, top mystery content unmistakable just to your fans on Facebook includes a feeling of restrictiveness and having a place. Posting information or goodies that couldn't be discovered somewhere else gives a specific impetus to the fans, and it can even make them feel exceptional.

#12 Ask questions!

How about we let it out. There's one thing regular among Facebook users, the reality they want to give their voices a chance to be heard. When influencing posts, to take a stab at joining questions or reviews. Only a suggestion, however. Keep the inquiries straightforward - nobody needs to round out the SATs on Facebook.

13 Lights, camera, YouTube! Don't limit yourself to pictures.

Recordings have insane high commitment rates so use them in your posts to get some genuine attention. Make beyond any doubt to get the right ones, however - those with just the right amount of entertaining and the right amount of "I'm attempting to make a point" in them.

CHAPTER TWO

Facebook Advertising for Everyone's Success

Facebook is the principal source of marketers for advertising in making traffic on their site. It's the well known and perfect social system platform. In which, creating content is the best system for Facebook advertisement tools. You won't burn through cash for your campaign. Most entrepreneurs used it as their phase to achievement in making a lead generation. Your needing traffic on the newsfeed of your business page? This is the right activity. This social media platform needs you to succeed. Five dollars ($5) is the assessed spending plan for each campaign, and this incorporates a variety of data, particularly your adaptability and target period.

This tool is the most confided in a supplier of advertising and lead generation for Facebook achievement. Programmed advertisement streamlining, transformation following, profound revealing, and news highlights are the fundamental part of advertising. The power of Facebook Ads is currently unfathomable for a marketing campaign in the present generation. It very well may confuse and convoluted. However, Facebook made it simple for their users. Advertising on social media is only the start of your essence on the web. Keep in mind, that in doing your ads, you have diverse gatherings of people. Make announcements that are identified with your business product, and target the right benefit. Even though Facebook started Lead Gen ads, you won't interface straightforwardly to your CRM. You have to download it physically.

Facebook gives a tool that provides aftereffects of the promotion and advances the criticism before going life it is designated "Imaginative Hub." It will enhance the media and gatherings cooperation. People use social media all the more frequently for their own and profiles data. Likewise, Facebook's give tools for outlining your profile pictures, and it encourages you to have greater commitment and benefit. People use social media as their platform for keeping up the connections and learn new things. In such a manner, Facebook additionally gives wellbeing and security of their products, which is the users. Indeed, you read it right. We the users are the products of Facebook.

Advertising on Facebook has the two (2) tools; it's the Ads Manager and Power Editors. Ads Manager is a tool that let you made and advance the campaigns. It is your organizer to the advancement and advertisers campaigns of the administrations. It additionally produces potential customers. Power Editor is the second tool. It used by the accomplished advertisers for their Ads administration. Means less common component it will leave befuddling. It has little particular changes in making an advertisement campaign. Observe; Ads Manager let you alter even various in the meantime. It would seem that as power editor. Power editor is speedier, and it is a superior tool to use.

While breaking down the advertisement campaigns execution is an absolute necessity. Expansion of sexual orientations, age, nation, gadget, platform, and time is the better path for less cash spent. Facebook presented overlays of elements ads for the groups of onlookers. Facebook covers, infographics, introduction, announcements, and cards are the most loved for visual substance. It will give more benefits and requests. Facebook will empower the users of advertisers in information buying to advancing their campaigns for their target benefits. It will decide the ads are creating deals. Amazons and Google are the most contenders of Facebook. The objective of Facebook is to assist their shoppers with having the right market and target. Facebook has expanding products and locating the right groups of onlookers because of the people that are currently more frequently to sign in. Dynamic ads help to elevate the product to convey in a right people.

Facebook is going out on a limb of setting up itself to rise into a shopping outlet. It trusts that they have the one of a kind shopping world, and just about 2 billion users are refreshed with regards to their social media. Facebook needs to demonstrate that they are not merely the base of all the marketing channel. It made a new buy purpose and thought additionally up. Facebook has a more critical way. More customers currently depend on Facebook as their shopping store. In which, Facebook has dynamic ads for a visual, and elevate the products to the people who have an enthusiasm for your image. The happiness of Facebook is very astonishing and fascinating, and it stays under strain to accomplish more. The activity of the people is matter and do their obligations.

Why Internet Marketers and MLM Are Moving Their PPC Campaigns to Facebook Advertising

This section clarifies how Facebook Advertising Beats Google AdWords PPC Marketing Face Down. Smart marketers are swinging to Facebook advertising as an undiscovered source of cheap and super targeted traffic.

Following quite a while of caution, some best search engines have now slapped the rears of well more than 12,000 internet and system marketing bodies whose records have been handicapped - forever! There's no legitimate purpose given - only an email saying diversion over. In any case, smart Pro marketers like our individuals aren't freezing - we've generally had a backup plan in a hurry.

Try not to Put your Eggs in One Marketing Basket.

Our recommendation has dependably been straightforward - don't put all your investments tied up on one place! In case you're utilizing Pay Per Click

Advertising, at that point make beyond any doubt you likewise attempt other PPC advertisers and have a reasonable piece of SEO going on too to produce natural traffic. A web optimization natural truck is driven by sheer diligent work - composing articles, discussion posts, web journals, Squidoo focal points, center point pages, video marketing - to develop your online nearness and mastery for your picked specialty keywords. Natural requires significant investment. So if you don't have the persistence and need to produce heaps of traffic quick, PPC is a good one to have as a vital aspect of your marketing model. Internet marketers and PPC specialists are tired of the arrogance of a portion of the PPC organizations. So in case, we're not doing PPC ads at the search engines, where do we get the majority of traffic we are as yet ready to create every day? Two sources.

Content Rich Social Marketing

There are heaps of approaches to creating free traffic from social system marketing. It's not by any stretch of the creative energy free obviously, as you do as a rule need to invest masses of your energy physically composing duplicate and making digital broadcasts and video marketing. Time is cash what not. Regardless of whether you outsource, duplicate journalists for your specialty won't come modest. So this natural SEO inviting traffic sets aside opportunity to develop and requires regular day by day exertion.

These regards add to your marketing blend, however, won't give you fast traffic. What's supercritical too is that natural SEO content is at last still controlled by the search engines, so these organizations still have power over how you get seen by your prospects. How hard is it nowadays to do what's needed smart catchphrase research to get your one of a kind specialty and rank on page one of the critical search systems. Relatively unthinkable - particularly in case you're one beginner endeavoring to contend with the enormous masters in internet marketing or MLM organize marketing field.

Advertising on Facebook

What company is reasonable and rational, adores subsidiary and internet marketers? What company pulls in about 40 billion perspectives every month and the traffic is uber quality and bargain basement? Who is this company? It's your well-disposed neighborhood... Facebook! Facebook is the leading company that Google recognizes is a genuine contender for them. Do you realize that Facebook has around 40 Billion users - that makes it five times the measure of Google! However, Facebook ads speak to only 5% of the advertising done on Google. Presently don't think Facebook is just for youths! Insidefacebook.com distributed its insights and demonstrated that lone 11% of users are matured 13-17. While 33% are 18-25s, an incredible 18% are grown somewhere in the range of 35 and 44. That is 100 million people! Also, a further 9% are aged 45-54 and 4% 55-65. Try not to go through another penny with Search Engine PPCs till you've looked at Facebook Advertising.

Why Facebook is the New Face of Paid Internet Marketing

Facebook is practically undiscovered contrasted with Pay Per Click on the real search engines. It's a "resting mammoth," a quick source of traffic that is...

- Significantly greater than PPC

- Less focused than PPC

- More targeted than PPC

- More affordable than PPC

What's more, in addition, Facebook's coordinated individual profiles implies you can home in on precisely the statistic you are attempting to target - by your keywords, as well as by age, sexual orientation, area, leisure activities, interests, instruction - it's basically amazing how profound you can get into -

giving you enormous decision and blends. Because of this, Facebook enables you to use a similar advertisement in various ways so you can indeed hit the problem areas of your users and their interests. Envision having the capacity to target by age, sexual orientation, film interests, AND keywords... you can genuinely hit your message home. So what this implies by and by is that the snaps you get on your Facebook advertisement are tremendously more targeted and change over far superior and cost far not as much as what you'd accomplish on say Google AdWords. If all that targeting wasn't sufficient to persuade you, here are some more advantages of utilizing Facebook advertising:

- Facebook is likewise excellent for beginners. It's straightforward to use and to set up your campaigns. If you can send an email, you can do Facebook ads.

- Facebook ads work in any market and will give a better ROI than PPC, notwithstanding for member marketing.

- Facebook advertiser rivalry is insignificant right now, so this is the ideal opportunity to take advantage of this massive source of traffic.

- Facebook ads can fuse the standard features, keywords, and body promotion yet also pictures, finishing what you can right now do with search engine ads.

- There's almost no loss with Facebook advertising since you can recognize super targeted prospects who officially inclined to your offer.

Following the Facebook Rules

There is a drawback. Facebook is gigantically defensive of its users. So you need to contemplate and take after their principles honestly. What's more, this will take you some time. There are three fundamental principles to comply. The dependable general guideline comes from what is designated "consent marketing." So make beyond any doubt you look at this, so you don't get your record dropped. The second key thing is to keep away from unessential, stun strategies and to use good sentence language structure. At last, cash making 'get rich snappy' plans won't be permitted so you'll need to get innovative about how you show your business opportunity basing them around marketing preparing or frameworks offers.

New Facebook Advertising Tools Can Maximize Social Marketing Success

You're a little startup. You have to develop your business and grow your client base rapidly without spending a considerable measure of money. Online is unquestionably an incredible approach. However the reliable techniques - show or hunt ads - shift extraordinarily in cost, administration time, targeting capacities and results.

Another positive focus for web-based promoting is web-based life destinations, for example, Facebook. With more than 500 million dynamic users, Facebook can be a potential goldmine for independent companies to reach new clients. On any given day, the more significant part of its users sign on to cooperate with friends, play diversions and post content, which converts into more than 8.3 billion hours multi-month spent on the friendly community.

This article wouldn't center around Facebook 101 - that is, setting up a static page, developing your friend's list, posting content and impacting out information and offers to your devotees. These can be viable. However, they target people you know or who know you, and possibly a little level of people past your quick circle.

Remembering the real objective to reach a more extensive audience, you ought to genuinely think about advertising on Facebook. Late changes in Facebook's advertising stage have made it more ground-breaking than previously and significantly more straightforward to use - at the same time giving you more noteworthy control over audience targeting, and advertisement spends.

Facebook has extraordinary targeting abilities and enables advertisers to reach people based on sexual orientation, topography, marital status, time of day, training and fundamental profile information. In any case, the mystery sauce behind Facebook's promotion stage is a "Suggestion Tool" that enables advertisers to reach people based on different interests and information that its individuals share. It works by examining and inventorying piles of information created by the whole Facebook people group, giving you better targeting power and the capacity than penetrate down profound. It additionally brushes the entryways off Facebook's past endeavors at targeting (e.g., nonexclusive channels, for example, "18 to 24 guys"), which could rapidly consume your budget and not convey the audience you require.

How Do I Begin?

First, you need to ask yourself - who is my audience? What sorts of people am I attempting to reach, and who might be most intrigued by my business? Targeting and timing are necessary for progress, and that is the place the Suggestion Tool exceeds expectations.

For example, a great companion as of late began an individual culinary expert business as an afterthought, targeting caught up with working families in Silicon Valley. For $50 in addition to the cost of perishables, she would plan and serve a gourmet supper at the customer's house. At first, she began with a basic Facebook page and started reaching out to her friends, associates, and previous partners.

she before long realized that she required somewhat more reach and began advertising. Utilizing Facebook's Suggestion Tool, she focused on wedded; profession arranged ladies ages 35 and up who lived in more well-off zones of Silicon Valley. She timed her ads to show up in the mid-to late-evening when these ladies started contemplating supper gets ready for the family. On the simple first day her ads ran, she procured two new clients, and in the long run, she quit her day occupation to seek after she recently discovered vocation full-time.

Making And Managing Your Ads

As a private venture, chances are you, and your workers have your noses to the grindstone every minute of every day, and are wearing many caps - none of which say "Official Facebook Advertising Campaign Manager." Fortunately, Facebook makes it simple to deal with your advertisement campaign. With a self-guided interface, Facebook gives tools that let you set every day spend budgets, dissect how your ads are performing, and deal with the recurrence of your ads so you can adhere to your budget.

The way to effective Facebook advertising is having moving images and duplicate that pull in the user's eye-all things considered, what great is having pinpoint audience targeting if your ads are fair?

Because images represent half of the real estate, it's essential to attract the user's eye to your promotion and motivate them to click. Reviving your real estate (e.g., turning your images) will expand your chances that a given model will resound with the people you're targeting. Contingent upon what number of ads you run, Facebook offers a mass image uploader with the goal that you can invigorate your images to your heart's content.

You ought to likewise take a stab at changing the promotion duplicate as regularly as conceivable to keep it crisp, with messages that address your different audience targets. Making an advancement or markdown offer will boost them to click on your ad...or even better, to call. Counting a telephone number on your advertisement is perfect for benefit businesses, similar to handymen, fitness coaches, mechanics and others for whom having an inside and out Website isn't essential to their business.

While this sounds awkward, the exertion could settle abundantly. Facebook's examination tools can reveal to you which images and duplicate reverberated best with which audience fragments, enabling you to spend more money on the ads that are producing the most outcomes.

Valuing

So what amount is this going to cost? That is the $64,000 question. Not at all like show or inquiry advertising, where you're bidding nearby content, setting or watchwords, purchasing advertising on Facebook gives you a chance to buy audiences. The more critical the audience, the higher the cost. Enabled to miniaturized scale target audiences with the Suggestion Tool, chances are thin that you and another advertiser will offer on precisely the same profiles.

Besides that, Facebook gives you the adaptability to set your promotion budget. You can spend as meager as $1.00 a day. Notwithstanding, all together for your ads to be viable, they should be seen. The higher your day by day advertisement spend, the more probable it is that your coveted audience for the day will look at your ads. You can't beat Facebook's accuracy showcasing - particularly amid subsidence.

Facebook Advertising Tips That Work

When you are burnt out on endeavoring to promote on Google AdWords and just losing money, it may be time to try Facebook advertising out. Notwithstanding its childhood, Facebook is developing rapidly. Advertisers are revealing a decent number of transformations originating from their ads running on Facebook, which is a positive sign. This implies there are loads of benefits accessible to the individuals who need to reach out and take them. Here are three simple tips that you can use to ensure your Facebook advertising turns a benefit.

So what precisely would it be a good idea for you to do with your Facebook activity once you get a few? You ought to send it to a landing page, yet what sort of landing page would it be a good idea for you to use? The fan page you made on Facebook! The truth is out: you can expand your changes by sending your site activity to the fan page you've made on Facebook. Loads of new advertisers don't yet realize precisely how gainful it very well may be to send business to a fan page. On the off chance that you use your site rather than the fan page, you'll see that the CTR and besides the transformation rate is lower. Facebook users are more OK with fan pages because it is less demanding for them to click the "like" tab to demonstrate that they are a fan.

Your shot for transformation is better with a fan page because you can cooperate with them by and by there. The more people you get to your fan page the happier you are. Use this procedure, and you'll see with your own eyes how well it works out. Facebook advertising wouldn't have the capacity to draw in the advertisers they do if it was impractical to focus on your market audience. You can take advantage of these gatherings and bring a high reaction because these people are energetic towards that specialty, which improves the probability of them clicking on your promotion frequently. In case you're a beginner, at that point you ought to pick up something about composing PPC ads, or ordered ads, and afterward work on keeping in touch with them. The best approach is to introduce your advantages so people feel them however much as could be expected. So the key to lifespan with your ads is to have a convincing and substantial duplicate that proselytes well.

How about we not disregard watchwords and getting the most out of your campaigns. You'll be throwing your net dreadfully wide if you construct your campaigns in light of statistic criteria. There are a couple of events when you can securely target fully. However, they are likely not the standard. You can diminish click costs by targeting littler specialty markets with catchphrases directly as you do wherever else. When you're advertising on Google AdWords, your advertisement is given a quality score to ensure it's sufficiently important. Facebook's calculation isn't as refined as Google's; however, regardless it has code that takes a gander at pertinence. The more significant ads you use for your Facebook advertising, at that point the better they'll perform - everything considered.

There's no motivation behind why try not to have the capacity to see positive comes back from Facebook advertising. From multiple points of view, this is much the same as composing grouped or PPC ads, and it's you do robust statistical surveying. If you are a beginner to IM or Facebook advertising and have little involvement, at that point, you will do fine as long as you approach this as a genuine business activity.

Facebook Advertising Strategy - Learn How to Advertise on Facebook

Actualizing Facebook advertising technique can be a compelling method to drive traffic to your Facebook page and increment your brand's permeability on Facebook all in all. Anybody can agree to accept Facebook advertising - you don't just have a page to do as such - and there is no set cost for an ad. Instead, you determine a most extreme sum that you will spend on the ad, either on a "per click" or "per thousand impressions" premise. As it were, you can pay each time somebody clicks on your ad or for every thousand times that your ad appears to a Facebook user. You can likewise decide the amount you need to spend every month on your ads, which can be up to $30,000. To the extent placement goes, Facebook shows your ad in places where it is logically essential to the topic of the announcement. This could mean setting it close by profile pages, pages, or on groups. For example, if you offer expressive dance shoes, your ad may show up on a Facebook page for an artful dance school in your general vicinity or in the ad space of the profile of somebody who has a place with a move academy. Whichever page it appears on; your ad will dependably appear on the right-hand segment. Contingent upon the page, up to three ads may appear on the double; in these situations, where more than one ad appears, it's unrealistic for you to decide whether your ad looks in first, second, or third place.

Facebook ads are generally best when their fundamental point is to drive traffic to a company's essence on the webpage, (for example, its page) instead of to offer a product or inspire people to the company's external website. For example, instead of directly advertising your website or blog, you can create ads for a particular occasion your company is sorting out and after that connection the advertisement to the occasions tab on your Facebook page. By and large, likewise with other web-based advertising, the more firmly related your ad is to the goal page a user arrives on in the wake of clicking on the announcement, the more effective your ad will be. Facebook advertising likewise enables you to target your ads, so they seem just to the group of onlookers you determine, for example, those of a specific age or in a specific geographic location.

Your Facebook and will create the most return if you ensure you're presenting it to people who are well on the way to be occupied with your brand, product, or administration. Although demonstrating your ad to anybody on Facebook may produce a considerable measure of impressions, the proportion of clicks to feelings won't be high, and the cost of your ad in respect to the arrival it persuades is probably going to be high.

Luckily, Facebook makes it easy to target your ad to particular groups of users through ad targeting. Once you've created your ad, Facebook will give you a few decisions about the groups of users you need to see the ad. You can target your ad based on a wide assortment of factors, for example, the user's age, gender, geographic location, or training level. You can likewise target your ad to show up for certain watchword ventures, and you can decide regardless of whether it ought to be appealed to people who are already fanatics of your Facebook page. Based on the criteria that you select to target your ad, Facebook shows you an estimated number of people who might be presented to your ad. From this number, you can evaluate how much running your ad will cost.

Your Facebook and will be more potent when you utilize targeted ad copy in conjunction with Facebook's statistic targeting highlights as plot above. For example, if your ad is aimed to ladies between the ages of twenty-two and thirty in San Francisco, saying their age group, gender, or the city of San Francisco in the ad copy itself will influence the ad to copy more pertinent to the people seeing the ad, which makes it more probable that they'll click through to your ad's goal URL.

If you find that in spite of choosing targeting criteria your ad is still failing to meet expectations, it might be that the target group you've selected is excessively tight. You can deal with this issue by broadening your targeting criteria, for example, extending the group of onlookers from San Francisco residents to all users in California.

The Pros and Cons of Facebook Advertising

Facebook has achieved a prevalence of extremely extraordinary extents with its number of users which is estimated at roughly 400 million and is developing once a day. It can likewise be expected that a more significant part of the everyday users on the Internet has Facebook accounts.

Due to this ubiquity, it has turned out to be inescapable for web business people to create a Facebook account, trusting that a more significant part of their potential clients is additionally on Facebook every day. Also, because of this conviction, it has turned out to be unsurprising for them to place advertisements on Facebook given its enormous notoriety.

Facebook paid to advertise can be a that great method for advancing products and administrations since this is the thing that advertising is, getting your products known to a decent number of people and at a snappier time conceivable. Paid advertisements on Facebook can better affect the people you targeted to.

The experts in Facebook advertising can be numerous, and the ad cost is one of them since you don't need to spend much in cost per impression in Facebook. Cost per click and even cost per print in Facebook are indeed much lower contrasted with the other system paid advertisements.

One advantage of Facebook advertising additionally is that you can pick the sort of people you need to see your ads. Their advertising stage can be based on watchers' age level, gender, instructive accomplishment, interests, different preferences, and other people related factors.

Since ads on Facebook are based on people-related factors, the impacts of your ads on your potential watchers can be more profound and most engaged in trust and certainty. This factor can profoundly affect your brand, and regardless of whether you can't get potential acquisitions quickly because your brand already has changed people, potential deals will come later.

Since people who are on Facebook, for the most part, don't have expectations of making buys, your ads might be some aggravation things to them, which can be a disadvantage. One approach to counter this recognition might be to create ads that are not "excessively pushy" and might be merely making leads.

Since Facebook is a long range interpersonal communication site people are just mingling, and the vast majority of them will be killed seeing advertisements flying up. You must be extremely imaginative in your ads and influence it to give the idea that you are not advancing excessively and lead them to your fan page where they get data and different things they can have utilization of.

There are significant advantages if you do pay to advertise on Facebook. Besides the capability of getting a high volume of traffic, it won't cost you much if you do a Facebook advertisement.

Does Facebook Advertising Really Work?

If you are searching for helpful ways to profit through the internet, you should begin acquainting yourself with how web marketing and web advertising works. As opposed to ordinary conviction, web-based marketing isn't only for established companies and large enterprises - because of the coming of social networking websites, one can without much of a stretch begin a business and manufacture a strong customer base in the blink of an eye.

One of the ordinarily utilized websites to maintain a business and engage customers is the ever prominent social networking website called Facebook. In any case, a lot of inquiries float around the idea of Facebook advertising: Does it honestly work? In what manner or capacity? Is Facebook advertising likewise perfect for new players in the business?

First of all - Facebook advertising works if all you are asking for is confirmation that you can be an active online advertiser utilizing the social networking website. Facebook functions as a result of the critical reason that it is a social networking website, a place where individuals uncover each information and unique insights about them.

Since Facebook users transparently share specific information about themselves, it allows online marketers and advertisers to design their advertising campaigns as per the taste and premiums of the Facebook users. The minute online marketers get hold of necessary market information, for example, age, gender, music inclinations, religion, political perspective, most loved pages, books, films, and so forth, they will have the capacity to make exceptionally focused on internet marketing campaigns.

To additionally see how Facebook works and why it is compelling, underneath is a portion of the advantages that Facebook can give any online business wanting to enter the Facebook market.

Facebook Provides Targeted Demographics

Around 97% of the Facebook users all around the globe uncovers their profile points of interest, including their age, religion, gender, and relationship status. At the point when online advertisers access this kind of necessary information, they can focus on the socioeconomics of their audience effectively.

Advertising and marketing turn out to be so substantially simpler when your intended interest group as of now uncovers such a significant amount about themselves. Facebook advertising gives advertisers a chance to center around particular people which augments the viability of your web-based marketing campaign.

Facebook Provides Instant Feedback and Direct Opinion

One of the numerous advantages of advertising in a social networking website, for example, Facebook is that you get the opportunity to see the prompt reaction and responses of the market in a matter of minutes. On the off chance that for instance another advertising campaign is discharged, you will promptly know the feelings of the market through the remarks, discussions, and refreshed status messages of the Facebook users.

Advertising in Facebook necessitates that you turn into a sharp onlooker and primary audience in the meantime. It is critical that you can read between the lines and break down the blended reaction and input of the distinctive Facebook users.

Facebook Advertising - A New Way to Level Up Businesses

The pattern of social networking has been generally recognized now by entire world. Amid the previous years, Facebook has been on the highest point of the opposition among various social networking destinations accessible on the internet. All through the world, Facebook has the most number of activity contrasted with different locales. With more than 500 million users, the site has been likewise utilized as a device for advertising. Especially in the United Kingdom, where there are more than 200 million users, a kind of Facebook advertising is an extraordinary way to advance one's business or occasion. Through Facebook advertising, a business can rapidly achieve each focused on market or audience. Advertising on Facebook can encourage people in the industry or companies to share their information and products by methods for interfacing with their correct purchasers relying upon their topographical and social data.

Manchester companies looking for a creative way of advertising their products or administrations should have a go at advertising on Facebook essentially in light of various reasons. It can superbly develop their associations with their customers by advancing their website or Facebook Page with only a single click on their connections, utilizing the "Like" catch keeping in mind the end goal to augment their impact and building a unified network inside their business fields. Manchester Facebook advertising can likewise assist them with managing their expenses or budget by setting a level of their daily budget that they are secure and alright with, modifying these expenses whenever of the day, and deciding to pay the administration when customers click or view their pages. Also, companies in Manchester can likewise pick among test images and content based advertisement to utilize and what will work for them.

Nowadays, individuals all around the world regard Facebook as a significant aspect of their lives, so companies will be anchored and sure that they are managing genuine customers having a genuine enthusiasm for their products. Advertising on Facebook can furnish companies in Manchester with CM Photographic that can distinguish the objective potential customers given their exact statistic.

It regards know a portion of the advertising strategies if Manchester companies will actualize this kind of advertising procedure. To begin with, they should figure out how to legitimately plan their advertisement. Transferring original information including fascinating titles and substance that will be incorporated into the body is an excellent way to begin. Second, companies must have the capacity to distinguish their particular audience as per their statistic information and ought to incorporate psychographic channels concerning potential customers. Next is setting up the campaigns and the price of the advertisement. Manchester Facebook advertising considers the amount as per sees, clicks, visit every day, and may set the calendar and budget every day. At long last, companies should audit their completed promotions, confirm the coveted budget, and check for wrong information. Manchester Facebook advertising system can give companies situated in the area an anticipated offer as indicated by their particular points of interest. Each company can direct and set its aggregate contingent upon the distinctive measurements and may rival others. Facebook can likewise give advertisers a lot of checking instruments with central advertisement manager area together with capable download information regarding any campaign each company is running.

10 Ideas for Marketing Your Business With Facebook Advertising

Facebook is considered the most famous web-based life arrange today. Its prominence stays to spread out with a need in web marketing where forceful and smart company proprietors and online marketers are sending Facebook marketing to achieve more target market as web traffic to their locales.

A more expansion to Facebook marketing is Facebook marketing that is developing well known where sure online marketing is targeted at particular specialty Facebook audiences that would profit the brand and company tasks. Facebook marketing consists of adaptable attributes that no online marketer or company proprietor may figure out how to keep away from today.

Facebook marketing consists of the ability to recognize a specific target market, track and determine the efficiency of picked advertisements, tweak advertisements in reaction to modifying market examples and customer habits. For the ideal results, online marketers and entrepreneur who partake in Facebook Marketing should utilize the accompanying ten impactful pointers.

Ideas # 1- - Have a Clear Objective

Each viable company needs a clear objective that may be achieved move the online marketer or entrepreneur. A fundamental goal may be set for pretty much nothing and brand-new organizations while more prominent market gamers would have more troublesome goals. The fixed objective would in all probability comprise of more web traffic to be delivered and more noteworthy sales that would expand main company concerns by methods for Facebook marketing.

A clear objective would assist online marketers or entrepreneur wind up being more engaged to use their vitality, cost and time painstakingly to appreciate ideal results toward the finish of the marketing project. While connecting with Facebook marketing if sufficient assets and know-how are expeditiously accessible, a company may be able to have more than a straightforward objective.

Idea # 2- - Identify Specific Niche Markets

Web online advertisers still need to decide their favored land spots to advance their brand and things rapidly, even though the world is their claim through contemporary developments today. New or little organizations should recognize a regional market that is more serviceable preceding widening past their viewpoints as they get to know Facebook Marketing.

As Web online marketers wind up being more gifted with the qualities of Facebook marketing, there is no outskirt to keep them down in connecting with worldwide and territorial customers on the Web for ideal outcomes.

Special web marketing projects may be set up with Facebook marketing to oblige the various customer prerequisites and modifying habits the world over.

Idea # 3- - Personalized Advertisements for Target Market

Web organizations require exceedingly specific audiences to be a hit. This would require a customized advertisement that arrangements with a particular gathering that would expand the marketplace nearness of the brand and things advanced. At the point when the friendly community accumulates suitable client info to assist online marketers in indicating the targeted audience for each online advertisement arranged and executed, this isn't any picnic for Facebook marketing.

A lot of fitting and excellent customer info may be gathered as a significant aspect of a dependable hunt making utilization of customers' age, sexual orientation, occupation, and interest. A blend of these necessities may restrict specific target audience that would flood up the advertisement achievement.

Ideas # 4- - Accommodate Existing Clients

One conceivable misstep of Facebook online marketers is a tendency to dismiss the existing in their franticness to search for brand-new planned leads. Online marketers must not overlook that without the current clients, their company probably won't be the place it is today. Existing clients should be esteemed consistently with fitting advertisements and exciting offers that would make them dedicated purchasers forever.

There is brilliant marketing power with existing shoppers who may be the brand's informal ministers from their entire satisfaction with the brand or company. More likely leads may come through from existing clients' contacts that would agitate more prominent sales for the business.

Idea # 5- - Realistic Budget Plan

Facebook marketing is vibrant with a spending plan that is versatile; thus, little or brand-new online organizations may set a littler estimated useful spending plan to turn on Facebook advertisement marketing on a littler measured scale till more incomes are made to permit a more significant extent of marketing on the Web.

More significant business with a bigger spending plan may pick more vibrant marketing advertisements that may expand various stages and channels for a more significant direct introduction of the brand and company to take pleasure in more significant returns. Ads may be run always or every so often relying on the set spending plan to make the needed outcomes.

Idea # 6- - Appealing Images Added in Advertisements

Images in advertisements tend to request more to audiences, relevant and especially engaging photographs that would create more interest and interest to trigger more unusual reactions. Online marketers may investigate different sorts of images on various advertisements to track their efficiency preceding utilizing the great decisions all the more regularly in future online advertisement marketing wanders.

Idea # 7- - Engage Facebook Advertisement Manager

No vastly improved gadget than the Facebook Advertisement Manager must be utilized to gather the necessary measurements on advertisement reactions for an exact give an account of the project's efficiency. Online marketers would be able to make more taught marketing decisions with the relevant info close by to avert restarting marketing blunders.

This would improve the achievement rates of Facebook Advertisements with the gadget administrator indicating facts about the publicizing effort, which empowers moment adjustments to the advertisements or modify the course of the marketing advocate higher efficiency.

Idea # 8- - Conversion Tracking Advantages

The use of Conversion Tracking controls reasonable JavaScript codes created on the business webpage to track web guests' actions and reactions. Such info comes back to Facebook where resemblance happens to supply an online marketer exact info about customer habits and assemble basic marketing info that would improve web marketing wanders.

Idea # 9- - Enhancing Facebook Posts

Expanding a Facebook post frames another component of Facebook marketing where the job is situated more noteworthy in the advertisement beneficiaries' News Feed zone to improve the chances of being seen. Any assortment of employment may be enhanced to improve the direct online presentation.

Idea # 10- - Add "Call to Action" Option

Each proficient marketing project needs to close with a 'call to action' which may close a sale where conceivable. This is the specific best completion line for a marketing project in spite of how vibrant the marketing technique may be. A call to action adds up to "Continually get a sale."

Facebook Advertising - Targeting Like A Sniper

Facebook advertising is in full impact at present. Sign in to your account, and you will be startled at how exact a portion of the ads are. On the off chance that you don't have an accomplice or if you look into specific things, Facebook advertising knows. This is awesome for advertisers as you can target by more particular criteria than any time in recent memory and split test until the point when you have the ideal battle.

How Do I Know If Facebook Advertising Is for Me?

Facebook advertising PPC is extraordinarily high, and there are numerous ways you can approach it. There are the paid ads, and after that, there is the free technique. Much the same as in Google, you have the paid results (AdWords) and the organic results (Search Engine Results Pages).

Organic Facebook Advertising

Organic inherently implies that you don't pay for your traffic individually. There is no such thing as totally free, so you will even now need to pay for it somehow, be that as it may, you don't spend a specific price for every snap or per impression. Here is a survey of natural Facebook publicizing.

1. **Setting Up a Fan Page or Profile.** If you have a product or service, you can set up a Facebook fan page for nothing. On this page you can put anything from recordings to deals duplicate, product data, a connection to your website, or auction straight the page.

2. **Get Traffic To Your Page.** This is the dangerous part that many individuals new to the web or marketing overlook. When you have the page setup, by one means or another you need to get traffic to it to see your great page and Facebook advertising data. There are such a significant number of ways of getting traffic. However, they all incorporate putting a connection someplace on the web that you trust people will tap on to get to your page. Once more, there are a large number of spots where you can put your connections;

anyway, a few places will help you more than others. This requires a great deal of manual work; writing articles, blog remarks, discussion posts, informing conceivable customers or other time to expend errand, well justified, despite all the trouble be that as it may if you are searching for lifespan in your business.

Paid Facebook Advertising

Paid Facebook advertising is the place the genuine players are and is the place you ought to go if you have a financial plan for advertising. These can be the ads that fly up as an afterthought or the ones that show up in the news source. There are various reasons why this is such a decent way to publicize. However, it costs. This is only one more advertising stage like Google and Yahoo or some other means of purchasing traffic, and utilizing this technique accompanies numerous favorable circumstances.

1. **Targeting Like A Sniper.** With Facebook advertising, you can focus on your correct customer, much the same as a rifleman would concentrate on his target. Facebook advertising PPC empowers you to target by

age, sex, likes, training, religion, ethnicity and a large group of different factors. This is the targeting that most advertisers dream of.

2. **Pay For What You Want.** When you are merely beginning another product or website and you don't have the deep pockets of Saatchi and Saatchi, you can purchase as little traffic as you need. On the off chance that you are just trying out another product or website to check whether you can make some money, Facebook advertising is an extraordinary way to go. You can get some traffic for $20, track it and perceive how it performs, and afterward, make a choice to either change your offer somewhat or take a stab at something different.

3. **Get In Your Customer's Head.** At the point when a user is looking through their Facebook account, they are in a condition of high fixation (even though you probably won't trust it). This is something of a habit for many individuals, and they are in a kind of daze, like TV seeing. At the point when your customer is in a modified state, for example, this, it is the ideal time to pitch your message to them. They will be online for some time and

regularly don't set a time constraint for Facebook. You can perceive what your customer likes and set your battle as needs are.

4. **Make Instant Business Decisions.** If you are anticipating utilizing SEO or organic Facebook techniques, it very well may be months before you have any information or traffic to make choices from. Utilizing paid Facebook advertising enables you to get some traffic who are now hot prospects, send them to your offer and see what happens. In 20 minutes you could as of now have sent 100 people to your suggestion, have the information and either change your opinion, proceed onward, or if you are profiting, scale it up and bank some excellent benefits.

Numerous people fear paid to advertise since it appears squandering money. This is a limited comprehension of the way toward putting resources into your business and isn't substantial in the marketing world. Each and everything you do toward your business costs you your time or your money. If you are out there writing articles, a blog is remarking and gathering posting, and you are investing your energy. If your time is $25 every hour, you could have labored for one hour and afterward sent that $25 of traffic to your offer and you can have some moment input as opposed to holding up months to check whether an offer believer.

Facebook Advertising PPC - Say Yes To 1 Billion Customers

Facebook PPC (Pay Per Click) is a genuinely compelling marketing methodology that you should set aside the opportunity to figure out how to utilize effectively so you can get your business into benefit rapidly. With more than 900 million users in all nations, it appears to be ludicrous not to use this stage to target your optimal customer. The extreme measure of data you can use to stamp your socioeconomics implies that even a nearby manufacturer in the nail clean industry can utilize Facebook advertising to pull in customers.

The Sudden Rise of Facebook Advertising Price

Facebook advertising is a standout amongst other ways to guarantee consistent traffic to your website. This is the thing that makes your image, organization or service surely understood and prevalent everywhere throughout the informal community market. The plan being utilized in this kind of advertising is that they will present to you the next market and targets the ideal people given your favored criteria, for example, their geological area, sex, age, and association where they are productively engaged with.

As far back as the start or propelling of Facebook way back in 2004, Facebook has turned into the most needed and visited free community media of a large number of users worldwide. This is the principle motivation behind why numerous advertisers are currently exploiting the site to publicize their products.

Advertisers utilize their particular prevalence for advertising advancing their products or services in Facebook. With this, Facebook has turned into the most loved spot among the marketers and online business visionaries. Advertising on Facebook is less demanding to do and costs fundamentally lesser, notwithstanding while putting their business profile over the site. Facebook advertising price is modestly contrasted with old daily paper ads, TVs, magazines, and even online advertisers. Facebook has surges of advertisers contributing on the social site these days.

Because of its consistently expanding fame, productivity and convenience everywhere throughout the world, Facebook advertising price has grown by 74 percent after over four years of being the world's biggest social market.

As per the most recent overview of TBG Digital, a free marketing firm concentrating via web-based networking media, Facebook advertising price presently shows charges per 1000 of impressions going up to 45 % crosswise over UK, France, Germany and in the US. This is because of the way that Facebook currently has ruled the interpersonal organization marketing area and quickly developing advertising fields notwithstanding outperforming Google.

Investigation reports from TBG and Effect Frontier demonstrate that cost-per-clicks ads drastically expanded by 22% from April to June this year. This depended on the 200bn promotion impressions in three months, from 167 users.

Even though Facebook ads like navigate rates have expanded its market spending plan, Facebook advertising still stays far superior to the current pennant promotions.

As per the result of the eMarketer, Facebook revenue has ascended to 104% which is 3.27 billion lower than Facebook's first estimation of 4.05 billion on 2011, yet two times higher than the Facebook revenues of 2009. This decay from its initially assessed future income during the current year did not consider the general wages of the business of Facebook.

Measuring the changes between different services and Facebook Ads, despite everything you're in an ideal situation with Facebook even at a marginally higher rate. This change demonstrates that the internet based life industry is a dynamic power that runs with the consistently changing tide of our world's economy.

Is Facebook Advertising Free With No Hidden Charges?

Facebook realizes that the issue of trust is a critical component in person to person communication. So when some individual asks, "Is Facebook advertising-free and with no shrouded charges by any means?" they can be extremely pleased to answer yes to the two inquiries.

Regular, Facebook has a stunning development of people originating from various areas, affiliations, societies, traditions and additional ways of life everywhere throughout the world. There are more than 800 million clients who are currently partaking in talking, sharing, rejoining and hunting down a few friends or missing relatives. More than 250 million people regularly go online to the social network to manufacture linkages with other people the world over. If you can tap these millions of users as potential customers, you will positively be astounded to discover that your brand or company can turn out to be progressively rough one day after another.

Knowing how large your objective market populace can be, it's anything but painful to think of a conclusion that posting ads on Facebook ought to be costly. If that is the situation, the inquiry "Is Facebook advertising free?" probably won't have been asked by any stretch of the imagination. Luckily, Facebook offers both paid advertising and free advertising of your business wherever you are on the planet, and gives you a choice to limit your conceivable target markets.

Both small and big-time businesses make their names prominent online by advertising their brand or company over the most dependable internet searcher or some social promoting sites like Facebook. Advertising on Facebook is one way to connect millions of people utilizing Facebook. Although Facebook users don't typically visit the website for purchasing something, they are powerless to everything new or stylish that they could discover on Facebook. If your ads can catch people's eye and light their advantage, they will probably join the horde of people seeing your page to look at your products' dependability and quality.

Hings being what they are, is Facebook advertising free? Advertising industry does not have something free. Be that as it may, when advertising on Facebook you can take the easy way for a base expense or you may need it your particular manner free of charge. Agreeing to accept another record on Facebook for individual purposes is altogether free. In any case that you need to have a page for your business, you'll need to adopt the distinctive strategy.

Facebook page is the most magnificent moneymaking instrument that enables your business to help up its name with only a small expense. Facebook page, fan page or business page on Facebook is made for business purposes. If you need your brand to have a significant accomplishment on Facebook, the Facebook fan page is free to create. Advertising on a fan page is in any case, would require a few charges.

When you mean business, you can use your page for your business for free. Just post your substance about the product, administration, brand or company you are advancing and put a connection that will drive the movement straightforwardly to your particular website, business or company site. In any case, you can't expect a change if you have a bunch of friends on Facebook. Thus, what you need to do first is to make millions of friends. That is the time they can see your post every once in a while. You can likewise label them about your product so every time they open their records, they will know that they are additionally advertising your product on their dividers. If you are exciting, quality and dependable product, these people should prescribe them to their particular system of a friend and promote exponential development to your site's fame. Presently, is Facebook advertising free? The appropriate response is, in fact, yes, for the business page route, and no, for paid advertising plans.

Facebook Advertising Tips and Strategies For Your Business

Facebook advertisements have not just ended up being persuasive and without a doubt effective; advertising on Facebook is exceptionally fulfilling. This is mainly because advertising on Facebook gives you a decent chance to connect with millions of potential customers within a brief period. Notwithstanding, Facebook advertising may not be that straightforward. The way that your ad(s) connect with millions does not imply that you can anchor deals. The accompanying tips and methodologies should help you in utilizing a fruitful Facebook advertising campaign.

Ad Type

Facebook puts available to you the Ad Creation apparatus that you use in creating your business ad(s). You can create an advertisement for three purposes; to get more fans, to promote your posts or to guide Facebook users to your traditional business website. You need to understand that Facebook ads do not look at ads yet instead show ads. Facebook users visit the site to connect with their friends and not to shop. Your primary question while creating an ad should in this manner to connect with your devotees who happen to be your potential customers.

Image

Advertising with images has turned out to be the best way to advertise on Facebook. For sure, Facebook has an arrangement expressing that 80% of all ads put on the site ought to be in the type of images. It is subsequently extremely critical that you create an ad with a convincing model for the planned purpose. Your ad(s) ought to be striking as well as eye-getting and crown-pulling too.

Gathering of people

The way that Facebook is gotten to by millions of its users ordinary does not imply that you can advertise to one and all. Undoubtedly, Facebook users are from various foundations, have diverse interests and are of different age gatherings. You unquestionably can't promote to them all. You need to distinguish a particular fragment of Facebook users to guide your ad campaign too. Facebook gives you an instrument to determine what classification of users you wish your adverts to reach.

Posts

Aside from creating ads, another effective procedure you need to utilize when advertising on Facebook is to develop essential posts that your devotees can like, offer or remark on. In addition to creating jobs all the time, you need to promote your posts to make them live long in your supporter sustains.

Cost

Like with advertising somewhere else, advertising on Facebook has its cost even though it is exceptionally insignificant. This does not anyway imply that you can advertise in any capacity you can. You need to keep your advertising cost low by setting average day by day advertising budget. You need to detail off with a small however sensible advertising budget and increment the same while checking how your ad(s) performs.

Timing

Timing is exceptionally critical with regards to advertising on Facebook. Usually, information that more significant part of Facebook users gets to the site amid working hours and that is the best time to run your advert campaign. Contingent upon your intended interest group, make it a point to decide at what times they get to the site.

Checking

There is hugely no good reason to run an ad campaign on Facebook if you are not in a situation to screen how your ad performs. In addition to changing your ad at any rate following a half year, make effective utilization of Google Analytics to monitor ad execution. This is the primary way through which you will ready to know whether to fire your campaign or utilize additional money related assets.

Facebook Advertising - The Secrets To Success

With over a billion enrolled clients and tallying, Facebook has gradually changed from a straightforward social site to one of the biggest advertising stages you can envision. You approach some instruments that empower you to advertise your business to a great many potential customers you can depend on to prevail in online marketing as far as the expanded probability of anchoring deals for your product(s) or service.

Fruitful Facebook advertising includes a number of a few fundamental advances, and the first of these is enlistment. Regardless of whether for personal or business, utilization of Facebook requires that you enlist with your email address and a watchword. This is in addition to other your particular points of interest. It is merely after active enlistment that you can approach Facebook. It is from your personal Facebook page that you can make your business page where a few business devices are put available to you.

The second means to effective Facebook advertising lies in picking up a reasonable number of friends or followers. You have to understand that fruitful advertising on Facebook isn't tied in with making direct deals, however, making connections first. All that Facebook is about is relationship marketing. It is like this important that you pick up a reasonable number of followers before you set out on advertising your business, product(s) or service. The advantage of having a fair amount of friends or followers lies in the way that they will have the capacity to comment, share or like your business, product(s) or service once you present the same.

The third step and which is presumably the most important one is in making your business Ad(s), product Ad(s) or service Ad. This you can do by influencing the utilization of Facebook's Ads creation to instrument accessible to you. Making content-rich posts about your business or product is additionally essential. Since you already have a reasonable number of friends or followers, they will have the capacity to share, comment or like your ads, activities that have the beneficial outcome of promoting your business and drawing in more followers.

Even though the over three are the most significant advances you have to take after to advertise your business on Facebook effectively, there are substantial issues you have to chip away at to prevail in your Facebook advertising endeavors. The first of these is to comprehend your target market. You genuinely need to characterize your target market following the few targeting factors that Facebook offers. Such targeting factors incorporate area, age, and enthusiasm among different variables.

A second issue you have to consider is the size of your advertising spending plan. It's a well-known fact that thousands have spent a considerable measure of cash advertising on Facebook yet have neglected to acknowledge advertising achievement. It pays to set a Facebook advertising spending that you can serenely oversee. The perfect situation is to establish a long haul advertising spending plan (paying little respect to how low it might be) instead of spending a critical sum within a brief timeframe.

Advertising on Facebook requires that you intently screen the execution of your advertising campaign(s). Since you may not make any deals toward the beginning of your advertising campaign, it is essential that you screen the number of fans, likes and comments that your advertising draws in. Visiting Facebook's Ad Report Area gives you the chance to download three critical reports; responder profiles, responder socioeconomics and advertising execution.

Step by step instructions to Create Successful Facebook Advertising

Facebook advertising is an adventure whose destination is Success. To achieve that destination there are choices to make and tasks to master. Pick one, how to begin. Which of the three current approaches to utilize Facebook will you choose?

Facebook for business just - Facebook Business account

If you utilize Facebook for the administration of your business pages and ad programs, you may choose this. There are upsides and drawbacks in this decision. If you already have a Facebook personal profile account, you have already rejected this choice.

Facebook Personal Profile for private utilize - Business Fan Page for business

Joining business use with personal contacts may not be something you need to do. The appropriate response is a Facebook Fan page. The power of business just fan page is the manner by which it opens up your store, products, and services to the world past your Facebook friends.

Facebook Personal Profile for business and Facebook Business Fan Page

This is the choice of expanding intelligence between your business and the world.

With that choice made, you are headed. Presently come some energizing and basic tasks to master.

Advertising with Facebook Task - Targeting

This is the first experience with the power of advertising on Facebook. You choose who sees your ad programs utilizing keywords and factors covering each part of eight hundred million Facebook clients. Your task is mastering the meaning of your market. The better you achieve this task, the higher the reaction to your advertising campaigns. This might be the perfect time to approach the specialists to enable you to point your target dead focus at the target pinpoint center for your market.

Advertising with Facebook Task - Attract and Engage

This is the point at which you encounter the control and adaptability of advertising with Facebook. Your task is guiding targeted guests to precisely what part of your advertising campaign you need them to see.

There is an extensive variety of choices, both inside Facebook and without. Guiding guests to your Facebook pages increases your ad campaign viability consequently. Another book on advertising with Facebook will clarify this procedure, covering Events and Promotions.

The second piece of this task is connecting with your customers. Your advertising objective is advancing substance and esteem valuable to your customers. By building trust, you manufacture a relationship more profound than business to the client. There are numerous approaches to advance substance and manufacture confidence now. Your task is figuring out how to compose Facebook advertisements with the most transparency and productivity.

The following tasks you learn while in transit to effective Facebook advertising are planning, and testing advertisements.

Advertising with Facebook Task - Budget Development

Compelling advertising relies upon aggressiveness of your keywords. There are two cost models. Ad programs begin by offering and planning.

CHAPTER THREE

Is Facebook Advertising Free for All Users?

By one means or another, if one log in to his or her Facebook account, he or she can't resist the urge to see the segment committed to advertising. So you ask, is Facebook advertising free? If not, what amount does it cost? On the other hand, each business expects to augment benefits and limit cost. Advertising has a place with the cost side. Thus, however much as could be expected, each company will search for the best advertising bargain that can be portrayed as "value for the money."

All in all, is Facebook advertising free?

Since Facebook propelled, it's in every case completely free to make an account on it. In any case, advertising and advancement is an alternate story. Facebook ads are a paid service. When you advertise your product, image, company or site, you will spend a day by day budget per campaign you made. It is dependent upon you if you will utilize the cost per click or CPC service or pay per 1000 impressions.

If you are sure on what service you will take for your budget in each campaign you post, you can make an Ad for your business or product. Select your most final offer per click if you choose to get CPC. Set your greatest day by day campaign budget and the number of clicks or impression that you will pay regularly. For example, you are paying for $0.50 per click, and you have picked up the new lead, you are paying $5.00 per lead cost.

In Facebook advertising, the private venture can increase the vast majority of the use. They can likewise drive activity for their particular website for free by utilizing the Facebook page. If you need to be visible in the floods of each user account, you need to advertise your product or services on Facebook. How are you going to?

Here are the straightforward tips on the most proficient method to advertise on Facebook:

- Think about what product you will advance.

- Create your particular account. If you are already in the Facebook, make your page for your product.

- Make a title of your Ad that can catch everybody's eyes.

- Make the substance of the Ad short and succinct. Make beyond any doubt to make content pertinent to what you offer.

- Put a picture that is additionally fitting with your product.

- Then pick the payment. It could be on CPC or Pay for the impression. There is a default sum recommended by Facebook you can transform it to lower or higher your offer keeping in mind the end goal to attract more Facebook users.

Returning, is Facebook advertising-free for every one of its users? Indeed, a wide range of advertising is not by any stretch of the imagination free. It includes a few fees and different costs. If you endeavor to take a gander at it, the measure of introduction you and your company or brand can get from only an essential Facebook and is amazingly high, which makes the fees moderately negligible contrasted with common advertising frameworks.

Since Facebook is online networking connecting more than 800,000 people the world over, your advertisements can end up viral to reach Facebook users. Each time potential clients "like" your Facebook ad, it will wind up visible to every one of his companions who should "like" them. Subsequently, the rate of your notoriety will take off exponentially. The main concern is, asking "Is Facebook advertising free?" is a decent begin for a business to consider doing showcasing on the web. Since you know the choices, it's a proper blend to go for free and which is Business Page creation, and if you have the budget, add the paid alternative too.

What Makes Facebook Advertising Different?

Google may have made more incomes before yet Facebook is overwhelming them. Facebook is utilizing an alternate advertising methodology not the same as different sites.

We should investigate what makes Facebook advertising unique and why they have expediently created 500,000,000 enlisted users overtime outperforming built up advertising organizations. Why has Facebook turned into danger as a business picking up excellent quality?

Facebook is utilizing the social chart or exercises to target people. Google then again enable users to position or direct their needs through particular terms or questions.

Google advertisers pay to be advertised; Facebook advertising is diverse because it enables advertisers to comprehend their audience. Facebook is at present utilizing people's likes and interests. Instead, Google employs keywords.

There is a 1:20 critical contrast in the cost an advertiser has utilizing Facebook over Google. Envision the reserve funds.

Google together with the advertisers relies upon keywords which are substantial conduct to attract an audience. The majority of Facebook users are enlisted and sincerely give out immaterial data about them which is then utilized by Facebook to help advertisers to attract their objective watchers.

Since the audience in Facebook gives data on their interests and advertisers can readily offer a product coordinating these, advertisers can then viably provide their product with secondary clicks, in this manner, lesser cost. The advertising for Google then again is search-based, so they need to type in keywords in the search engine and execute a lot of clicks before the ad rises.

Google utilizes Search Advertising rather than what Facebook employs which is Display Advertising. Google enables a user to search keywords while Facebook matches the keywords to a man's likes and interests and shows these emerge advertisements before the user.

Indeed, you may not by any means discover all around focused AdWords in Facebook however you will dependably discover a tailor fitted advertisement at the sidebar. Facebook advertising is diverse since it utilizes clear socioeconomics to attract a particular user barely.

Google is made into a pay-per-click (PPC) advertising so the advertisement can be seen one-time just when the search engine is utilized. Then again, there is a propensity for users in Facebook to in the long run observe indiscriminately through advertisements since as an informal communication site, users may see your publication as often as possible, so advertisers need to make or outline numerous ads or change their ads various occasions.

There might be a few gatherings where Facebook advertising may not work but rather as a general rule it is exceptionally successful for the vast majority since it is precisely focused on that the advertisers dependably get the exact sort of people clicking on their advertisements. This new technique for advertising is hitting great insights and another incentive to the two users and advertisers.

Facebook Advertising on Weekends: Is It Really More Effective?

People in business who use Facebook for their ad campaigns are continually searching for more ways to advance their business utilizing this social networking site. Facebook is home to very nearly 1 billion subscribers from all parts of the world. Besides people, Facebook likewise goes about as an information mediator amongst superstars and fans, businesses and customers, groups and individuals, and some more. Advertising on Facebook is esteemed to be incredibly compelling the individuals who took a stab at utilizing it revealed a 30% increase in their income.

If you have been utilizing Facebook to advance your business, you are presumably thinking about whether different ways can enable you to help the number of your page's devotees. One prominent thought is that ads that keep running amid weekends are more viable than those that are flashed amid the weekdays. Intriguing, would it say it isn't? You need to find out if this claim is valid, read on.

The Myth: Weekend Advertising

As an ever increasing number of people find the advantages of utilizing Facebook advertisements, an ever-increasing number of studies and examines are being led to enhance the consequences of these ads. One of these new ways is weekend advertising. Weekend advertising works on a fundamental idea: the number of Facebook users is substantially higher amid weekends, which empowers people in business to target a more significant number of people and allure them to purchase from their website.

The weekend advertising principle is additionally valid for other social networking sites, for example, Twitter, Multiply, and Tumblr. A place called tweetclock.net, detailed that the number of people who log in their Twitter accounts is 40% higher on weekends than on weekdays. Analysts mirror the same on Facebook.

Given that, weekend advertising is a genuinely basic idea that independent ventures can use to help support their following on Facebook. In any case, one question remains, is it mighty?

The Proof

An examination led by TBG advanced, a social media examiner, inferred that advertising on Facebook amid weekends is to be sure more compelling than advertising on weekdays. The exploration board examined somewhere in the range of 66 billion impressions which are recorded for a variety of three months. Their examination discovered that ads play out their best amid Saturdays and they are even from a pessimistic standpoint when Monday comes. The normal for Saturday is 12% higher than the Monday normal.

TBG Digital concentrated the click-through rates which are closely corresponding to the cost per click of an ad and also its cost per impression. Ads which have a higher CTR are demonstrated all the more often while those with a low CTR must have a higher offer to be flashed as every now and again as the others. In any case, another way of driving a higher CTR is to plan their ads to appear amid weekends when the number of potential clients is higher.

Simon Mansell, TBG's Digital CEO said that the reason for this conclusion is that weekends are by and large designated for unwinding and available time. People who are out of school and workplaces find the time to get up to speed with their social media life and in this way, are probably going to run over an ad or two. Another reason is that people who use Facebook amid weekends tend to focus on their News Feed since they get to Facebook amid their breaks. On weekends, they have more opportunity to meander through the site, and they tend to see ads and click through them.

By and by, I surveyed 100 Facebook companions and made a similar inquiry. These 100 people hail from no less than five nations and every ha a way of life to some degree not quite the same as the others. Shockingly, just 26 said that weekday ads work better for them. A portion of the reasons they gave was:

- Access through Facebook is through workplaces and schools amid weekdays

- Weekends are for destroying and investing some energy in the family

- Computer support and repair are by and large done amid the weekdays.

The rest of the respondents said that weekend ads work better for them since they have more seat time spent on the page which allures them to click an ad. Likewise, the more prominent dominant part said that they have more opportunity for Facebook amid the weekends than on weekdays.

The Ad Campaign

These examinations don't guarantee that you can most likely get a lift for your income when you apply the weekend ad hypothesis. Remembering the real objective to abuse this principle, you need to ensure that your ads are sufficiently striking to grab the eye of your targeted crowd. Likewise, make ads that are a long way from the normal and conveys the message in a primary yet powerful way.

If you deal with a fan page for your business, posting announcements, photographs, and others on your page amid weekends is probably going to attract people to your business page and become acquainted with additional about your item. Connecting with your fans in a fundamental incidental data question can likewise attract them to your site.

The weekend ad principle is observed to be more powerful for businesses that target children and youngsters. In any case, utilizing your particular extraordinary brand of innovativeness and, some assurance, you can use this principle to turn your business into the business that everybody thinks about.

People in business who use Facebook for their ad campaigns are persistently searching for more ways to advance their business utilizing this social networking site. Facebook is home to very nearly 1 billion subscribers from all parts of the world. Besides people, Facebook additionally goes about as an information mediator amongst big names and fans, businesses and customers, groups and individuals, and some more. Advertising on Facebook is esteemed to be exceptionally compelling the individuals who had a go at utilizing it announced a 30% increase in their income.

Set Facebook Ultra-Targeting To Work For You - Facebook Advertising Basics

Considering getting a portion of those 400,000 eyeballs per day that log onto Facebook an opportunity to take a gander at your advertising? Better believe it, I don't blame you.

Facebook is without a doubt the best advertising chance to tag along in a long time...no...make that tag along ever on the web! I mean a significant portion of those 200,000 people who log on day by day even stay for a spell, giving advertisers fair chance to get their adverts seen, and ideally reacted to.

If you are contemplating utilizing Facebook advertising, here are a couple of pointers to remember:

1. Know And Follow The Rules

Disrupt the guidelines, and you could have your ad yanked, and lose cash. Ensure you acquaint yourself with Facebook's advertising rules, to maximize your advertising budget.

2. Getting Your Ad Approved

Facebook favors each ad before it's run. They disapprove of advertisements for 'get rich fast' plans for example, additionally ensure your ad is family inviting, this is Facebook for the love of God, my kids log on day by day! The endorsement procedure can be conflicting, however, so if your ad is opposed once you could resubmit it and it could be affirmed later...btw.

3. A Picture Is Worth A Thousand Words

Most Facebook ads have a picture obliging them and in light of current circumstances. It's been demonstrated time, and again a decent relative picture will get your ad seen by more people, and reacted to more regularly than without a photo. Attempt to find a film that isn't just pertinent to your offer, yet is eye getting too.

4. Target Your Audience Precisely

Facebook enables you to target the individuals will's identity presented to your ad unequivocally. This is something to be thankful for (a standout amongst other reasons to advertise utilizing Facebook) and will enable you to get a higher CTR (click through rate) and ROI (degree of profitability.)

This will enable you to limit those presented to your ads until the point that you are getting the understandable best outcomes. You can, for example, target a group of people who are companions of the individuals who 'loved' your ad. See the intensity of this? The individuals who have demonstrated an enthusiasm for what you are putting forth are just about as 'targeted' as you can get.

5. Watch out for Your Costs

Similarly likewise with AdWords, it very well may be anything but trying to let your ad costs make tracks in the opposite direction from you. So watch out for your offers, clicks, and results, to remain inside your advertising budget.

Once your ad is live, you can adjust your offer to get the exceptionally least expensive clicks, or impressions possible...I always keep a close eye on my ROI to continue my campaign operating at a profit.

6. As Always Test, And Test Some More, Tweak, And Tweak Some More

Facebook gives you a tremendous amount of information on your campaigns, so you can adjust, and change them keeping in mind the end goal to get the most value for your money. Because of the idea of Facebook targeting, you can part test, and streamline your ads, and gathering of people to get each click feasible for your advertising dollars.

The ideal way to find out about advertising with Facebook is to go ahead finished and run a campaign or two. Get your feet wet, take in the framework and use the brilliant advertising opportunity Facebook offers to your online business.

Using Facebook Advertising - How It Can Help You As A Marketer

A great many people realize that Facebook advertising holds immense potential to acquire a considerable measure of new businesses. Be that as it may, they straightforward don't know how precisely to do it right. You find keeping in mind the end goal to take full advantage of Facebook you need to know how to use the intensity of Facebook the right way to develop your business whether it be online or disconnected.

There is enormous potential for utilizing Facebook to advertise however most advertisers approach it from the outlook that they are only "giving it a shot." That isn't sufficient to end up victorious in a marketing campaign on Facebook.

Understanding Facebook Advertising

Hitting the nail on the head could change your business rapidly from a little player in your industry to a noteworthy player. Be that as it may, sadly on the off chance that you miss the point you could be passing up a great opportunity the lousy influence of advertising on Facebook and waste your time as well as your most profitable asset in business-your money.

Business owners both online and disconnected are always seeking to extend their internet-based life reach. Be that as it may, what most business owners need is to figure out how to tap into Facebook.

So how can one precisely approach finding out about Facebook advertising? Some key components must be added to any Facebook campaign to make it successful.

Before you begin advertising you should realize that you need specific vital components, for example,

- **Super Fans:** What are they and why you need them

- Essentials of a Facebook marketing establishment

- Smart strategies that will grow a lucrative fan base-this implies not merely fans but instead fans that purchase and enlighten their fans regarding your product or service.

- Quick tips to get your fans discussing you, your product or service and get them occupied with what you bring to the table

- How to move fans up the positions to super fan status

These are the key components that you need to know to keep in mind the end goal to be successful with your Facebook strategy. Without see how to execute these strategies in your Facebook advertising, you are just dawdling and money. Furthermore, this will lead to disappointment and later abandoning Facebook marketing.

Once an advertiser comprehends the estimation of advertising with a medium that is as critical as Facebook, at that point they can start to tap into its great chances. Additionally, the esteem that Facebook offers far exceeds the benefit of advertising on Google pay per click.

Utilizing Facebook advertising as a here and now and long-haul strategy for developing your business is the best speculation that any organization both online and disconnected can put resources into.

Three Ways to Become Successful With Facebook Advertising

Facebook isn't only one of the present most prominent long range informal communication sites, but on the other hand is one of the world's best online advertising and online marketing devices. On the off chance that arranged deliberately and executed legitimately, your Facebook advertising campaigns will be a hit in no time.

Notwithstanding, Facebook can get a bit of befuddling sometimes particularly on the off chance that you are not that used to utilizing the site. That is the reason most specialists trust that the ideal way to hold a successful online advertising campaign on Facebook is to become more acquainted with the site first - know how it is utilized, how people use it, and what highlights it has that will enable you to reach your objectives.

The significant thing about advertising and marketing your products and services on Facebook is that you get a mighty advertising road for your business however without expecting you to pay several dollars. Advertising in Facebook is maybe the least demanding and the most financially savvy way of marketing a business online, so ensure that you are exploiting those advantages.

You want to hold an online advertising and marketing campaign on Facebook; there are a few hints and strategies that you can do to guarantee your prosperity. Here are the main three ways to be successful in Facebook advertising without needing to spend to such an extent.

Mix up your audience with unique offers and promotions.

You need to think about Facebook, the reality the people inside Facebook are there to have a great time, make new companions, or speak with old ones. People don't join to be shelled with a forceful marketing pitch.

If you need your ads to be exceptional, make it light and assault your market utilizing an alternate approach. Extraordinary compared to other ways to draw in customers is to offer different rebates and limited time things.

Encourage audience participation.

If you are running an ad campaign on Facebook, in all likelihood, your business additionally has a Facebook page or a Facebook gathering. Draw in your customers by influencing them to feel included; encourage audience participation in your Facebook page and request your fans or your individuals to share their musings about your business.

Customers like it when organizations or businesses request their suppositions and listen to them. Give your audience a chance to take an interest by making necessary inquiries in your page, or welcome them a decent day.

Reward customer devotion.

Beside feeling associated with the business, something else that customers like is being valued. Keep in mind that you are not merely searching for getting customers, you are after a steady stream of customers with the goal that your business remains successful for a more drawn out time.

Ensure you influence your customers to feel increased in value. Reward them with little complimentary gifts and advise them that it's your pleasure working with them.

How Does Facebook Advertising Help Your Site?

In no other online site is there so much relevant individual information being straightforwardly shared with people other than the most famous long-range informal communication site Facebook and an online advertiser, a shrewd one, would think that its difficult to disregard this marvels and use it to their advantage, make do with the abundant supply of particular information and information about people that would ordinarily take a bank to inspire a similar sort of information. Thus Facebook holds an extraordinary guarantee for online advertisers who need to play out a more intensive targeted showcasing on the internet. The Facebook ad program enables advertisers to hit the correct demographics based on by and by volunteered information, for example, age, interests, bosses, location even to the town, and even relationship status and companion's records.

The Facebook advertising program is similarly new, and so far master advertisers are still on an "attempt to get the vibe" mode making explores different avenues regarding the Facebook ads and perceiving how the targeted audience responds to the posted advertisements. Being new as it seems to be, even computerized showcasing specialists who are already exceptionally capable in expressions of the human experience of advanced targeting shows in paid hunt advertising are merely beginning to get their feet wet are still on the tweaking period of running their ad programs on Facebook.

In any case, there are already guaranteed parameters that you can use as an online advertiser to get your ads seen by the millions of Facebook users, and one of these strategies expects you to tailor fit your ads to work inside the Facebook general feeling and experience. You need to comprehend that the users of Facebook spend an extreme measure of time compared to the amount they pay in different websites and keeping in mind that on Facebook, they collaborate with companions by sending messages and ongoing visiting, share information, for example, photographs and recordings, and associate with their favored causes, yet never look for anything to purchase so their mentality isn't to spend yet to connect with people they know so on the off chance that you have this circumstance as a top priority, at that point you can create a sort of ad where you can painstakingly choose pictures, altering invitations to take action, and tweaking on the messages on your ad to take into account the ordinary air on Facebook and that is cooperation.

So most importantly, do whatever it takes not to consider Facebook a standard site like an e-magazine where you can just post your ads and drive the viewers into your website for moment activity, however for a couple of famous brands, this may work for any site they wish to post their ads on, yet since you are not them, it is smarter to stick to a more programmed fight plan and stick to the general Facebook experience because improving results. You can create Custom Pages as a significant aspect of your Facebook Page empowering your viewers to effortlessly "Like" your website so you can without trouble re-market to them with refreshes about new arrangements and forthcoming occasions later on.

2 Most significant Advantages To Facebook Advertising (And Why You Should Be Using It If You Are Not)

Facebook is known to have developed into the one of the biggest (if not the biggest) long range interpersonal communication sites on the Internet.

We should look at some intriguing measurements about this long range interpersonal communication site - It as of now has more than 500 million (and tallying) dynamic individuals around the world (If Facebook were to be a country, it would be one of the biggest nations on the planet - Ahead of countries like

Brazil, Russia and Japan!), and there are near a significant portion of a billion of dynamic users surfing and looking at innumerable number of pages on this one single person to person communication site day by day, for example, taking part in the different Facebook groups and share interests through this ground-breaking system.

The immense fame of Facebook has introduced numerous advertisers and businesses with an open door for them to make use of this stage to extend their business and reach out to considerably more potential clients around the world.

With regards to reaching out to potential clients on Facebook, the best strategy to reach out to several thousand (if not millions) of them quickly is to make use of Facebook ads.

There are numerous advantages to utilizing Facebook ads to advertise your business, items, and administrations, and in this part, we will share with you 2 of the most significant benefits of Facebook advertising, and why you ought to use it on the off chance that you have not already done as such!

1. Shoddy Advertising To A Huge Audience

Compared to advertising using Google AdWords, it is significantly cheaper to create and put advertisements on Facebook with Facebook ads (there are times where you need to pay pennies for a tick!)

The primary reason is that of the way that when compared to Google AdWords, the number of advertisers in Facebook advertising is considerably lesser. What's more, as a result, there are significantly smaller contenders competing for the advertising space accessible on Facebook, and accordingly, the cost of advertising is substantially cheaper.

2. Capacity To Target Audience Based On Demographics

Not at all like Google AdWords, where you target audiences based on the different watchword expressions (and countries and states you need your ad to show up in), with Facebook advertising, your target audiences based on demographics.

What's more, regarding demographics, you can target audiences based on:

- Location
- Age Group
- Birthday
- Sexual orientation
- Watchwords
- Training Level
- Work environments
- Relationship Status
- Interests (in men or ladies)
- Dialects
- Associations (to the different Facebook pages, groups, occasions, and applications)

With this alternative, you can genuinely pinpoint your targeted audiences directly down to the everyday detail. Furthermore, when you know who precisely to focus, you will have the capacity to experience exceptionally positive results from your Facebook advertising campaigns.

Would You Like Your Sales Message To Get In Front Of Over 500 MILLION "Hungry" Buyers Today?

Find Little-Known, Covert Insider Secrets That Will Transform Your Facebook Account Into An Income Spinning Asset - And Start Generating For You Massive Amounts Of Cash Day-In, Day-Out... On Complete Autopilot!

How to Pass Facebook Advertising's Strict Requirements

Facebook offers outstanding amongst other advertising programs out there. To begin with, you will approach more than 500 million users when you promote on Facebook. These people speak to a wide variety of ages and nationalities, giving you a differing gathering to publicize to. Facebook advertising is likewise moderately shoddy, particularly considering the way that you can laser target who sees your advertisements. You can choose your gathering of people utilizing a wide variety of measurements including age, sexual orientation, education, business, marital status, and catchphrases. Facebook advertising is incredible, yet they do have a stricter arrangement of rules and publication decides that you need to take after to get your promotions showed. This is the thing that you have to do to make beyond any doubt your promotions will pass their prerequisites.

In the first place, you need to be straightforward with your advertising. Facebook's advertising program tends to take after the site's general logic of being perfect, flawless and open. They will likely make advertising something that is straightforward and exclusively customized, so remember this when assembling your advertisement.

There are a lot of more stray pieces of things to consider also. To start, you need to run every one of your crusades from one record. When all is said in done, you can't open various documents to run numerous different battles from. You likewise can't robotize the production of advertisements except if you get express consent from Facebook to do as such.

If your advertisement has content of a URL connect in it, at that point, your promotion needs to link to that same URL. All users must be sent to a similar landing page, and those landing pages can't have a couple of things. They can't have any fly up promotions or the like on them, and they can't have any conduct that shields users from shutting the page effortlessly and without a problem. Nothing unforeseen can happen when a user endeavors to explore away from the page. The advertisements and the page that the promotions send users to can't make it appear as though Facebook embraces them in one way or the other. You can't use Facebook's logos or other recognizing data.

The promotions themselves must be related to and consistent with the page that they send guests to, they need to be explicit portrayals of what is being publicized and anything that is broadcast needs to be straightforwardly accessible on the site you assign users to. You can't make any absurd or unverified claims in the promotions, and the advertisements can't be constituted as badgering in any feeling of the word. There is likewise a wide variety of products that you can't offer through ads on Facebook. These incorporate things like obscenity, anything that is hostile or indecent in its language, anything with tobacco or weapons, betting, or any illegal action, to begin.

Generally speaking, a significant portion of the terms of use for Facebook advertising tends to be a pervasive sense. For whatever length of time that you are offering a real product legitimately and directly then you shouldn't have any issues getting your promotions endorsed.

The Other Side of Facebook Advertising

If we are to take a gander at the positive parts of Facebook, without a doubt, it is a hands-down victor regarding marketing on the web. In any case, the individuals who have attempted Facebook advertising before say that there is something else entirely to Facebook than what meets the eye.

Facebook is no uncertainty an excellent way to market on the web. Regarding the fame and permeability, it can provide for products, services, and websites. With just a little spending plan to sell and promote, Facebook is to be sure a good systems administration site to publicize.

What are the reasons why Facebook advertising did not work out for past users who have attempted Facebook to publicize their products?

To begin with, it is still new. Facebook has just been around for barely two years. Its maximum potential has not been found yet, and a portion of the highlights are new. Numerous marketers don't know yet how to use Facebook viable. Marketers are confined to a few highlights of the site which limits them to use it to its maximum potential.

Second, it's anything but a web crawler. It is just a web-based life organizing site which is just a piece of an entire framework. There are only two or three things that we can do. Different techniques together with Facebook Advertising ought to work keeping in mind the end goal to pick up progress.

Third, the use of a landing page. Facebook enables connections to be posted yet this is landing pages which are not suitable to use. We can make a page wherein there is a general thought regarding the promotions that we have posted on the said site.

Fourth, the inability to construct a list. What list am I alluding to? These are the lists of imminent purchasers. People who have interests in our advertisements ought to be followed up finished half a month. The support that interests to transform into trust keeping in mind the end goal to make them agreeable and make a deal out of it. It may seem like an exceptionally entrusting work yet those relationships would be a significant help in future undertakings.

Fifth, the inability to make propelled explore. It is critical that we recognize what and who are the target markets that we are going for. We ought to have the capacity to know where to discover them. We should remember their needs and have the ability to convey it to them through our products and services. We ought to likewise examine our rivals who are additionally utilizing Facebook as a way to promote their products.

Those were a couple of the common mistakes and disappointments in Facebook advertising. We should remember that even in Facebook, uniqueness matters. On the off chance that our product is novel yet it is sufficiently compelling to start the interest in our target market at that point most likely whatever difficulties we experience, we can outperform.

Our objective in Facebook Advertising is to stand out enough to be noticed, keep them interested, form trust and in the long run work with them. Along these lines, dodge these common mistakes with a specific end goal to accomplish and procure more in Facebook advertising.

Targeted Facebook Advertisements

With regards to advertisements, you mostly can't beat the capacity of Facebook advertisements to target your clients by the statistic. You don't need to stress anymore over choosing the correct catchphrase; you can focus your clients by area, age, sex, interest and even by where they work!

The potential of Facebook advertisements is enormous. With more than 400 million dynamic users there is a lot you can do with this advertising medium. An ever-increasing number of expansive organizations are beginning to promote here understanding the benefit of having the capacity to target such vast amounts of dynamic users.

To begin with, you can target your advertisements in the nation. Presently, you can do that with AdWords and other pay per click systems, yet the true excellence comes in having the capacity to choose urban areas to promote in. You can likewise have your adverts showed to people in a span of those urban communities as determined by you in miles.

This takes into account fantastically targeted advertisements, specific if you have a disconnected business. The incentive here is immense and could wind up being a miniaturized scale business in itself for some marketers who pitch this service to nearby organizations.

You can likewise target people by age. Keep in mind that Facebook stores a lot of data about its users and this is all to your advantage with regards to advertising.

On the off chance that you know about the age scope of people well on the way to purchase your product then you can show your adverts exclusively to them.

On the off chance that your product is related to birthday events you can target people on their birthday celebrations as well! How incredible is that advertising opportunity? A lot of people go to Facebook for their birthday events because they get lots of messages from people.

You can target people by sex as in are they male or female and furthermore whether they are interested in men, ladies or both. Add to this the capacity to target people based on their relationship, i.e., single, engaged, in relation or wedded then you have astounding advertising potential.

Would you be able to envision putting Facebook advertisements for wedding-related services to people who are engaged? Or on the other hand dating services to people who are single? Or on the other hand how to get a conning accomplice to people who are in a relationship? Or then again how to return the start into your contact to people who are hitched?

The acquiring potential is critical just from this.

Next, you can target people based on their language so you can genuinely promote privately based products and services in any nation.

Making it a stride facilitate you can mainly target people who have specific preferences or interests. This implies you could focus your reptile keeping product to any individual who has enrolled an interest in reptiles. Targeted advertisements like this are precious.

You can likewise target people based on their education and even where they have worked or are working. This gives immense potential in targeted adverts for education products or even employment chasing products!

At long last, you can even target people who have specific associations in Facebook, i.e., companions, or gathering enrollments. This encourages you much more to focus your advertisements to people with unmistakable interests.

The potential for Facebook advertisements is immense, and it is something that you ought to take a gander at to help your business. With generally modest advertising and exceptionally targeted socioeconomics, you can increase exact access to your target market. The chance to benefit is enormous, and it's developing each day.

Thumbs Up for Facebook Advertising?

Where to put your showcasing dollars can now and again be a test for entrepreneurs. Internet-based life keeps on being a channel many decision-makers question if the cost in time and money will create a beneficial return.

Facebook's argumentative IPO raised genuine discussion among investigators over the real value of the online life site to the advertisers that make up its primary wellspring of income. The contention rotates around information recommending that the percent of focused customers to click an ad on Facebook is even lower than the already low normal for web advertising on different sites. An ongoing Reuters/Ipsos ponder demonstrates that four out of five users surveyed said that they had never burned through money as the consequence of advertising on Facebook.

The low achievement rate of paid ads is an impediment that Facebook's administration still can't seem to survive, yet don't ignore the 150 million unique US users visiting the site in any event once multi-month to stay in contact with friends and family. That is half of America, and Facebook claims 900 million overall users in a universe of only 7 billion people. Never in history has it been so natural to reach (and become to by) such vast numbers of people. An ad's "lower-than-normal" hit-rate on Facebook could, in any case, mean a lift in deals.

This mid-year Facebook started enabling advertisers to purchase ad space specifically in user's news feed not merely on the right-hand side. These ads may demonstrate more successful as these accounts fall into the organic substance feed so consistently. For instance, if somebody prefers your organization's Facebook page, their friends may see a story about it in their news feed. By supporting the story, the individual's friends will probably observe it and wind up inspired by your items and administrations.

Although you might need to assess if burning through money on Facebook advertising is right for your business, you can at present create an organization Facebook page which costs nothing. Urge customers to "like" your page so they can get updates and fantastic offers straight from the source. Connect with these customers by posting content that they can talk about. Their association not just furnishes you with significant customer feedback, Facebook enhances its value by advising their friends that they like and care enough to collaborate with your business. At the point when users connect with you, make beyond any doubt to answer so they know you're listening.

Regardless of whether you choose to attempt paid advertising on Facebook, web-based life is setting down deep roots. Facebook is at present investigating additional routes for businesses to achieve customers in the future, so regardless of whether it remains the most significant name in internet-based life quite a while from now, except for the future of advertising to consolidate an ever increasing number of components of long-range interpersonal communication.

Facebook Advertising Strategies

The development of Facebook over such a brief period has been marvelous, and it currently gets a higher number of hits than Google. So for the individuals who are in business online, it is red soil. The free video workshop broadly expounds on the best way to set up your ads on Facebook, and especially what will be endorsed and what won't be. That will spare a lot of time and exertion

Remember that Facebook is most importantly a web-based life stage. The vast majority don't go ahead to

Facebook to shop. It doesn't care for e-straight in such manner! If you are expecting moment deals, you might be frustrated. What you have however is the chance to interface and build a relationship with your imminent customers, making the long haul "know, similar to, trust" relationship. As opposed to sending your prospect to a business page, send them to a squeeze page where you can offer them something of value in return for their points of interest to build your list. You can send them to the end of arrival straight after!

Or then again you can send them to your Facebook "Fan" Page where they can like your page, and you can utilize it simply like a squeeze page with a selection frame and build your autoresponder list. Regardless of whether they don't take your complimentary gift offer your fans all over book page is another list of prospects who have to some degree "picked in" to have more contact with you.

Try different things with your ads. Create more advertisements which are focused on fewer people. Split test the ads to perceive what works best. For instance, if you are advertising a locally established business would you say you are mainly searching for stay-at-home mums? Taylor your duplicate to that particular group of onlookers. The considerable advantage the Facebook advertising strategies have over Google is that you would laser be able to focus on your advertising as per the socioeconomics, interests, age, sex, relationship status and instruction that people put on their profile; and not merely the catchphrases and area that Google permits. It's been recommended that ladies will react better to ads with pink in the picture. With Facebook ads, you can give that a shot!

That aides especially with attraction marketing (see: Attraction Marketing Strategies of the New Rich), where you are situating yourself as an asset to help and give answers for people in your specialty.

Most users won't make a purchase right away, so you have to establish beyond any doubt that you are at any rate connecting with them. If you went out on the town and held up about fourteen days to get back to them, there most likely wouldn't be a second! Follow up with a message that gives away value to them. The more you give openly, the more you will get. The same goes for your fans. Follow-up with your fans regularly and reliably.

Being Consistent with Facebook Advertising Strategies. One thing an excessive number of web advertisers do is quit utilizing a strategy too rapidly before it has had an opportunity to work. This will apply to Facebook advertising strategies as well. While you will need to experiment with various

166

diverse ads to perceive what works best, split test them and inspect the details; you will likewise find that outcomes will change with mark mindfulness. Remember that law of marketing that people will regularly be presented to an item, or an advert, eight times before they make a move.

This implies doesn't spend past your methods for multi-week and have no money left toward the end. Instead, set sensible spending plans that you'll have the capacity to handle for longer timeframes.

CHAPTER FOUR

Passing the Strict Regulations in Facebook Advertising

One reason why Facebook was slung into the most mainstream long range interpersonal communication site that it is presently is expected its consistency with keeping up the general user experience and ensuring that all aspects of Facebook and everything that gets associated with it, including the ads, should add to the steadiness and consistency of the entire website setup and the creators of this wondrous social site have been without fall flat dedicated to securing the user experience by keeping the place spotless, steady, predictable, and free from misleading advertising and they can do this by passing the strict regulations on Facebook advertising. So the entire Facebook advertising setup is by and mostly relied on changing existing ads into more customized messages that are sliced to the shape and preferring of the individual users in light of how their companions connect with music specialists, brands, and every one of the businesses that are important to them.

So Facebook has set up an arrangement of guidelines that apply to all ads that will show up on the website and even those ads inside canvas pages of Facebook Platform applications and in addition to this, all ads are required to meet the terms of the Privacy Policy and Statement of Rights and Responsibilities meaning all advertisements are liable to the principles of Facebook and the website maintains whatever authority is needed to reject or expel advertising that they may consider as conflicting with the organization's ad approach. In the meantime, similar guidelines may change anytime, and Facebook can forgo any of the instructions composed at whatever point it needs in light of its attentiveness.

One of the strict regulations on Facebook advertising that an advertiser needs always to remember is that no one can make and additionally oversee distinctive Facebook represents the sole reason for advertising except if generally given the communicated consent by Facebook and in such manner, ads that contain a URL or an area name in the body must connect to a similar URL or space, not to any outside website. In the meantime, presentation pages are not permitted to generate pop-ups, and this incorporates pop-unders and pop-overs, when a user enters or leaves the site page, or mouse catching where the advertisers don't enable the users to use their program back catch and traps them on the site abandoning them nothing to do except for "x" out from the entire place inside and out.

Before an ad can force a watcher to click on an ad and submit relevant individual data, for example, date of birth, name, telephone numbers, standardized savings numbers, and whatnot, the advertiser needs to ensure that it is being done to empower a web-based acquiring exchange where the arrival ad page unmistakably and concisely demonstrates that an item is being sold. In short, hanky-panky isn't permitted.

Facebook Advertising Tips That Give Great Results

Web-based advertising has hugely developed over a previous couple of years. While Google indeed pushed advertising over the web, the most up to date passage is Facebook. Advertisers are discovering that Facebook is hugely viable for focusing on specific specialty markets and groups of people. In this article, we will discuss three brilliant Facebook advertising tips that will direct you amid your campaign.

You should chip away at checking your ad campaigns on Facebook deliberately. One thing that everybody experiences when they start to advertise on Facebook is that the execution goes down after some time. What influences this to happen? It's mainly because the cost that you bring about to connect your focused on users on Facebook increment with time. Necessarily, this implies the people that are the initial ones to click on ads will, for the most part, do this with a significant portion of the ads. In this way, once you are done with the principal group, the cost to converse with the others will keep on growing. This is the reason you should watch your ad's click-through rate all the time. Decide the click-through rate of your ad. When you begin to see the execution lessen, switch your ad or change your outside group. Honestly, every ad has a life expectancy, and after this life expectancy, they are not viable. So to get more from this life expectancy and get more out of your ads and lower your financial plan, this particular advance is imperative.

The following suggestion will necessitate that you give us some due and tune in to our experience. When making any ads, for the pictures of any people in your ads; you will need to have horrid people in them, or to a high degree lovely people. This works mostly because people react to anything that conjures compelling feelings. At any rate, remember the ultimate objective to get the best reaction, the appearances in your pictures must not be even the slightest bit fluffy or out of core interest. All you're endeavoring to do, in addition to the enthusiastic reactions, is to leave people speechless when they see your ad. This approach fits in well with users on Facebook because users are molded to taking a gander at appearances of people. Right? Right.

When you're utilizing Facebook ads to direct people to your fan page, ensure you're sending to the custom tab, as opposed to your wall.

Nobody has control over wall content, for obvious reasons on the off chance that you know anything about Facebook. You realize what shows up on the custom tab, where you can pass on a solid deals message or request that they make a move by preferring your page. Wall remarks can get uncertain, as you surely understand, and that is the issue with sending your fans to your wall. It has for some time been appeared, even in a short timeframe, that when people arrive first on your wall, the transformation rate is lower. So it's simple... send people you need to work with to your custom tab and not the wall.

All things considered, from the above article we arrive at the end that Facebook advertising is, in reality, developing step by step and with a specific end goal to receive the most in return, you need to be a savvy advertiser who knows how to use broad testing and different systems to make a campaign useful.

Facebook Advertising Essentials - How to Profit From Facebook Paid Advertising

You have the best ad copies for the different items and administrations that your website is putting forth. You know it's great because you had it tried it and retested with your advertising campaigns. Presently you think you are ready to put it onto Facebook's advertising campaigns. Be that as it may, how might you make a profit from your ads on Facebook?

In the Internet world, there are heaps of various ways to set up your advertisements. Standard ads, Google AdWords, Content Network, and so forth are only a couple of cases of ways you can advertise.

You may inquire as to why put a paid ad in Facebook when you could put your ad copies elsewhere. The appropriate response lies in the notoriety of Facebook. Indeed, you could put your pretty much anyplace. You have all the flexibility to do as such, however, will it have the traffic it so merits?

At Facebook, one is ensured the traffic of individuals and non-individuals alike. It's the most mainstream networking site as of right now, and you wouldn't have any desire to miss the potential market drifting in this site. Individuals always check their pages planning to locate some well done. Your ad may get a click or two right after you post your ad onto the website.

Your little venture of ad costs which exceed the potential profits you will make by having great ads that change over well.

Keep in mind the business standard of spending more to have the capacity to profit more. This ought to likewise be your mantra when you are putting your ads on Facebook. This is the means by which one makes the profit out of Facebook paid to advertise. The second profit-production rule needs to do with the clicking part of Facebook advertisements.

When somebody clicks on your ad, they will naturally be re-coordinated to your business page, which could, in the long run, be transformed into genuine customers who will buy whatever it is that you are offering.

How Facebook Advertising Can Effect Your Business

Facebook advertising is a first showcasing apparatus that can be used by anyone. It is available to everybody who will get into business interpersonal interaction. Utilizing Facebook ads is an effective way of getting some presentation over the commercial web center, and numerous business proprietors have already demonstrated that. Through the best possible use of Facebook ads, a significant increment in customer-base and deals can be watched.

Things being what they are, do you maintain your very own business? On the off chance that honestly, at that point don't give yourself a chance to get left behind. Here is a portion of the accepted procedures you can do in getting the best outcomes out of Facebook advertising.

The principal activity is making your Facebook ad. Think about a snappy title for your ad, something that is 25-characters long including spaces. At that point, type the substance for the body of your advertisement. For this part, 135 characters are the farthest point for the length including spaces. To make your ad additionally engaging, it is best that you upload a picture that impeccably suits the message you are passing on in your ad. Following that, you will be asked whether you need people to be diverted to your particular webpage or a Facebook page, application, group or occasion. In addition to that, you will likewise have the opportunity to accurately focus on your audience by age, sex, area and that's just the beginning.

Mostly, those contain the simple strides of making Facebook ads. Be that as it may, as you are doing as such, you need to remember what your advertising objective is. What would you like to concentrate more on: getting traffic to your Facebook page/claim webpage or making your ad unmistakable to whatever number users as could be expected under the circumstances?

If your re directing people to your page is more critical, at that point selecting a compensation for each click ad is suggested. Along these lines, you can make sure that your ad is exceedingly focused to the most appropriate and fitting audience. Be that as it may, for this to be conceivable, you need to have a greeting page which can either be your Facebook fan/group page or your very own separate webpage.

When you are influencing your image/to organization's name effectively unmistakable is of higher significance, the better decision is the pay-per-impression type of ads. By settling on this type of Facebook ads, it implies that.

How to Reduce Your Facebook Advertising Expense

If you have an Internet business, it is more probable that you will put resources into advertising on the net to guarantee that you will accomplish the success for your business. Facebook advertising is an excellent way to achieve this business success, thinking about its abilities to cover a broad reach, with its a huge number of dynamic users.

So if you advertise on Facebook, will it cost less as well as have more propensities to send people directly to your greeting page or fan page than sending them directly to your website. Also, through along these lines, it will probably hold your group of onlookers and gain their trust later, which can likely outcome to deals later on.

First you need to comprehend the contrast between advertising in Facebook with its cost per click (CPC) plan and cost per thousand impressions (CPM) contrasted with those ads with alternate systems. Along these lines, Facebook advertisements work on a stage that depends on the different socioeconomics of users of which you want to target as if you select to focus particular age levels, instructive levels, sexual orientations, or other user's specifics.

As already specified, advertising on this social site is so shoddy contrasted with the other ad programs in different systems, and you will see this if you attempt it the first time. Also, in this way thinking about its remarkable way of targeting users, you won't encounter it with whatever else on the web.

Anyway, by advertising on Facebook, you first toy with cost per click as indeed, it is substantially less expensive than the cost per thousand impressions. You will see this is additionally valid with ad programs with alternate systems.

By beginning off with choosing pay per click, Facebook will give you a suggested bid range with a specific sum. Try not to bid on the most minimal amount on the proposed bid range and run your ads.

You will see that your Facebook ads will have propensities to get affirmed gave you take after its rules completely. Once your ads are already running don't stop there, yet keep checking your, and if you end up mindful that you are not getting enough, then it is essential that you bid more.

In any case that you need your ads to keep up the lesser cost don't sit tight for Facebook to expand your suggested bid range which can happen on the off chance that you are not getting a significant change and Facebook will quit running your ads. When this happens, your suggested bid range will expand so before this happens you need to build you bid marginally higher than your first and run your ads once more.

Essential Rules of Facebook Advertising

Owning a small business implies having restricted assets for marketing and advertising purposes. Particularly when you are endeavoring to join the web-based marketing and web-based advertising amusement, one would quickly surmise that a business ought to have the severe canons with a specific end goal to remain above water the solid rivalry.

Be that as it may, there are right now new choices with regards to advertising an organization or a business online without spending such a significant amount on advertising and marketing. Today, you would now be able to exploit interpersonal interaction websites, for example, Facebook to enable you to promote your small business in significantly compelling ways.

Any new online advertiser would need to know the insider facts keeping in mind the end goal to give your Facebook a chance to page drive new customers. Maybe you have quite recently joined the site and are not yet comfortable with how it functions, which is the reason for promoting your business on Facebook appears an exceptionally overwhelming assignment.

Good thing the internet has become so user well disposed nowadays and websites likewise observed the requirement for them to be touchy to first-time users. Facebook is explicitly anything but trying to coexist with, and with the customary updates and changes in its plan and format, one will quickly get the hang of exploring on Facebook in no time.

In any case, say for instance you don't have that little additional time amid the day to take a seat before the PC and figure out how to experience Facebook, how are you going to promote your business successfully on it? The following are a portion of the essential systems that will help any new Facebook user support their business in the website adequately and reasonably.

Adhere to the straightforward and take things moderate.

It is difficult to get results medium-term, and it will doubtlessly require an investment before you can develop the lingering returns, yet that does not imply that you surrender immediately. A ton of Facebook advertisers confers the mix-up of giving an ad a chance to battle go because it didn't work following two or three days.

Try not to get disheartened easily. Adhere to the straightforward techniques first and take as much time as necessary with it.

Construct an individual association with your fans.

One drawback of promoting a small business on Facebook is the smaller fan base that you have. However, instead of crying and getting all baffled by the number of fans that you have, why not exploit the small amount and take advantage of every one of them directly.

Regardless that you are yet a developing association, it is always an incredible plan to collaborate with each new fan on an individual premise. Assemble an association with each fan, and they will end up being a fan and a customer for eternity.

Never spam.

Never spam your individuals or other Facebook users. Spamming is one sure way to erase your brand on the web for good.

Surefire Ways to Succeed in Facebook Advertising

Marketing on Facebook is getting higher and higher, and Facebook advertising has made its way into most web business people's brains as an extraordinary way of promoting items and make their businesses known to the entire world. With Facebook, a vast number of users and the idea that the more significant part of these users is signed on day by day, advertising on this online networking site can give your business heaps of success.

Accomplishing the success of your business by taking part in Facebook advertising should be possible in ways that you may have been doing with your other internet advertising programs. Be that as it may, here are different surefire ways to get this business success by doing advertising on Facebook and doing these ways accurately are essential.

With your advertising plan on Facebook, you need to spread out what is your objective in doing this advertising program whether you need to get to your intended customers or merely making your quality felt in the internet field. This is so because if you need your image to be known and your brand based on the internet, you can contribute progressively and achieve a good picture and make yourself known and can even give more advantages over the long haul.

If your goal is to contact your intended customers, you need to target these people effectively, too. With Facebook's novel methods for targeting customers, by way of the user's socioeconomics which is all in their database, you can have more extensive options of targeting customers which can be more intrigued or inspired to recognize what you offer.

Make your Facebook ads genuinely emerge and draw in watchers' consideration while in the meantime being particular and succinct in your ad message to extremely guide shoppers to it. Without overlooking the catchphrases, your target for the particular customers, you need to make these ads convincing and featuring your items one of a kind highlights can be like this of pulling in the watchers' consideration.

Utilizing an active call to activity expression can do well with your Facebook advertising effort and genuinely actuate watchers to make an activity promptly. A strong urge to activity expressions can be "click here," "get a statement," or basically "peruse" and these can be an inspiration for your customers to do what is said.

If your goal is to manufacture your image and brand on the internet, the utilization of an image and is beneficial for doing. An appealing and essential image can convey more advantages to your battle.

The straightforwardness in getting relevant data can shield your customers from getting exhausted, and when they click on your site, you will have increased beginning success.

Growing Your Facebook Fans Easily

Web-based life is so intriguing because a large number of the prominent channels travel every which way. Be that as it may, there are likewise some web-based life channels that have been solid since their commencement and they are significantly more grounded than any time in recent memory now. Facebook is one of those. It started out in a substantially more constrained path than it is presently and it is still imperative to become your Facebook fans for the advantage of your business and your brand.

The difficulties of Facebook

When you have a Facebook profile and you perceive your need to develop the number of fans that you have, that is sufficiently challenging. Then again, if you have made another page (for instance, another page for your brand), it very well may be considering all the more challenging. In the past, it might have appeared to be easier to get new fans pretty effectively and rapidly. The reason that you may have had that observation is on account of it was more comfortable.

These days, then again, it is significantly more troublesome. The explanation behind that is, basically, the volume of your opposition. The truth of it is that if you need to develop your fans (it is protected to expect that you are searching for top-quality, pertinent fans), it will take more effort and time on your part than it would have in the past. It's implied that you need to draw in your Facebook fans too. Now, you might get some information about achieving that.

Identify your target audience first: before you can do anything, you need to identify precisely who your target audience is and what they need and need. This needs to happen even before you start to utilize your Facebook profile to build your number of fans. You don't need or need everybody who is on Facebook to be one of the members of your target audience. It is essential that you comprehend that you should have the capacity to fathom the issues that your target audience members are encountering. If you can't do that, they are not your target audience members.

Utilize the most suitable voice: Once you have made sense of precisely who is your target audience members, the following thing that you need to do is to establish an association with them. If you don't start to associate with your target audience members, you won't have the capacity to develop a relationship with them. As you are presumably very much aware, the link is at the core of your ability to succeed. With regards to your content, you need to write given your target audience members. Your content needs to resound with your target audience. That is the means by which you establish a passionate/human association.

Draw in with your target audience members: When you are thinking about how to write your content, you likewise need to think about your condition. You need to consider how your content will influence people once it is housed in your specific Facebook page. You will see that a portion of your material works more viable than other content. If you have posted content and you understand that not very many (or no) people have read it, you comprehend that try not to post that kind of material since it isn't working for you. There are few unique things that you can post, and you will accomplish positive outcomes. Some of them are questions (provocative), intriguing photographs, articulations in which the target audience member needs to fill in the clear, and challenges in which they might want to take part.

You need to remain with it as long as possible: Although you will not have to invest a lot of money in your Facebook efforts, that doesn't imply that you don't need to invest anything. Your investment is as time and effort. If you wish, you can likewise spend money (as paid commercials); in any case, it isn't fundamental and, as a rule, you will find that you have spent money and those promotions don't yield anything. How disappointing is that?

Remain centered and inhale: As you are developing your fans, you should dependably remember to stay grounded. If you have any possibility of identifying with your target audience, you will achieve that by associating with them as one human to another. Your ultimate objective (similar to the case for everybody) is to offer your item or potentially benefit. Be that as it may, you can't be pushy about it. You need to build up the relationship with the other individual, invigorate it after some time, manufacture trust and believability, and after that, in the long run, the other individual will most likely need to purchase what you are offering.

Remain focused on your schedule: People love a program that they can rely on. When you focus on posting your content two times per week on certain days and at specific times, you need to stay with that. People are animals of propensity, and they depend on having the capacity to read your content when they anticipate that it will seem on the web. That isn't such a significant amount to ask (from their point of view), and it won't require a lot of effort on your part either.

Pay attention to the analytics: Analytics and measurements are essential for your business since they give you an unmistakable sign of how you are getting along and how you can enhance what you are doing. You will need to pay attention to particular things, and if those things are not working or don't appear to be significant, you should refocus your attention somewhere else.

CONCLUSION

Online life advertising and Facebook advertising is explicitly the advanced strategy for setting ads. This is in no uncertainty as a result of Facebook's millions of users who access the site every day. There without a doubt millions of businesses with a solid nearness on Facebook because of the way that advertising on Facebook is the most changing over advertising media at any rate with regards to online advertising. In spite of what many have come to think, advertising on Facebook isn't pure as it appears and this is the primary motivation behind why numerous business owners swing to online life advertising firms to make and deal with their ad campaigns on the webpage. There are positively numerous strategies you can utilize in advertising on Facebook. What you need to realize anyway is that every one of the procedure has one target; making of the successful ad(s) that offer. You may likewise need to recognize that every one of the policy points a sure something; to reach out to whatever number Facebook users as would be prudent. Reaching out to numerous Facebook users ought not to be your principal objective. You need to reach out to users better set to access your product/service. In reality, Facebook's advertising instrument is equipped for recognizing users who can profit by your business. Aside from guiding your advert(s) to a particular portion of Facebook users, picking your advert category is extremely basic. It is a category you choose that decides how your business and reaches out to your target Facebook users. Although the decision of division can be a test, you may need to realize that Facebook has an inbuilt robotized framework that gathers significant user information to generate higher ad income. Notwithstanding whether you embrace to post your ad(s) on Facebook all alone or draw in the service of an online networking marketing firm, Facebook puts available to you a standout amongst the best devices you need to use in dealing with your ad(s); the cost per click (CPA) apparatus. This is an estimating technique that empowers you to pay for a particular measure of clicks on any given day. You to be sure to have the choice of keeping up the traditional ad marketing on Facebook or the CPA program.

MARKETING YOUR BUSINESS COLLECTION

HOW TO DRIVE TRAFFIC TO YOUR WEBSITE

THE ULTIMATE GUIDE

Get 100,000 Visitors To Your Website In Less Than A Hour And Learn How To Drive Targeting Traffic To A High Converting Page And Make Money Online

WRITTEN BY

DALE CROSS

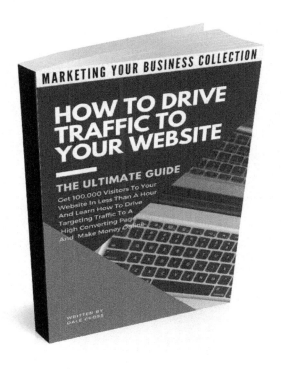

DOWNLOAD NOW YOUR FREE E-BOOK!

*Available on your free Kindle version or by
subscribing to dalecrossmarketing@gmail.com*

69651592R00109

Made in the USA
Middletown, DE
21 September 2019